T0312295

Cambridge Elements

Elements in Econophysics
edited by
Rosario Nunzio Mantegna
University of Palermo
Bikas K. Chakrabarti
Saha Institute of Nuclear Physics
Mauro Gallegati
Università Politecnica delle Marche
Irena Vodenska
Boston University

RECURRENCE INTERVAL ANALYSIS OF FINANCIAL TIME SERIES

Wei-Xing Zhou
East China University of Science and Technology

Zhi-Qiang Jiang
East China University of Science and Technology

Wen-Jie Xie
East China University of Science and Technology

CAMBRIDGE
UNIVERSITY PRESS

Shaftesbury Road, Cambridge CB2 8EA, United Kingdom

One Liberty Plaza, 20th Floor, New York, NY 10006, USA

477 Williamstown Road, Port Melbourne, VIC 3207, Australia

314–321, 3rd Floor, Plot 3, Splendor Forum, Jasola District Centre,
New Delhi – 110025, India

103 Penang Road, #05–06/07, Visioncrest Commercial, Singapore 238467

Cambridge University Press is part of Cambridge University Press & Assessment,
a department of the University of Cambridge.

We share the University's mission to contribute to society through the pursuit of
education, learning and research at the highest international levels of excellence.

www.cambridge.org
Information on this title: www.cambridge.org/9781009486613

DOI: 10.1017/9781009381741

First published 2024

A catalogue record for this publication is available from the British Library.

ISBN 978-1-009-48661-3 Hardback
ISBN 978-1-009-38173-4 Paperback
ISSN 2754-6071 (online)
ISSN 2754-6063 (print)

Recurrence Interval Analysis of Financial Time Series

Elements in Econophysics

DOI: 10.1017/9781009381741
First published online: February 2024

Wei-Xing Zhou
East China University of Science and Technology

Zhi-Qiang Jiang
East China University of Science and Technology

Wen-Jie Xie
East China University of Science and Technology

Author for correspondence: Wei-Xing Zhou, wxzhou@ecust.edu.cn

Abstract: Extreme events are ubiquitous in nature and social society, including natural disasters, accident disasters, crises in public health (such as Ebola and the COVID-19 pandemic), and social security incidents (wars, conflicts, and social unrest). These extreme events will heavily impact financial markets and lead to the appearance of extreme fluctuations in financial time series. Such extreme events lack statistics and are thus hard to predict. Recurrence interval analysis provides a feasible solution for risk assessment and forecasting. This Element aims to provide a systemic description of the techniques and research framework of recurrence interval analysis of financial time series. The authors also provide perspectives on future topics in this direction.

Keywords: econophysics, recurrence interval, financial time series, scaling behavior, multi-scaling behavior, risk estimation, early warning

JEL classifications: C41, C46, C53, G01, G17

ISBNs: 9781009486613 (HB), 9781009381734 (PB), 9781009381741 (OC)
ISSNs: 2754-6071 (online), 2754-6063 (print)

Contents

1 Introduction

1.1 Two Equivalent Questions

Black swans, gray rhinos, and dragon-kings are extreme events that are rare but ubiquitous in nature and human society (Sornette, 2009). Dragon-kings emerge due to an underlying mechanism that is very different from the driving mechanisms generating small, mediate and large events, are more predictable during their developing transient dynamics than at other times, and are outliers in the ubiquitous power-law or stretched exponential distributions of the bulk (Sornette, 2009; Sornette & Ouillon, 2012). It is of vital importance to understand the statistical regularities of extreme events and make a prediction for the next extreme event. In econophysics, there are elegant methods designed for the prediction of extreme events (extreme price fluctuations). For example, the log-periodic power-law singularity (LPPLS) models are very successful in the modeling and prediction of financial bubbles and antibubbles that could be positive or negative (Sornette, 2003a, 2003b). The LPPLS models aim at answering the following questions: (1) Can financial bubbles be diagnosed in real-time before they end? And how? (2) Can the termination (regime change) of financial bubbles be bracketed using probabilistic forecasts with a higher degree of certainty than chance? And how? (3) How can antibubbles be modeled and their future evolution predicted?

Alternatively, we can formulate two mathematically equivalent questions that are important to policymakers, firm managers, and market practitioners:

Question 1: Assume that a financial dragon king occurred at time t_0 and no dragon kings occurred between t_0 and the present time $t_0 + t$. What is the probability that the next dragon king might occur before time $t_0 + t + \Delta t$?

Question 2: Assume that a financial dragon king occurred at time t_0 and that no dragon kings occurred between t_0 and the present time $t_0 + t$. What is the expected residual time $\langle \Delta t \rangle$ to the next dragon king?

In Figure 1.1, we illustrate the schematic plot of the above questions. We note that the rich and complex behaviors of recurrence intervals are driven by the clustering or burstiness of the events defined. Indeed, if we shuffle the raw (financial) time series, we destroy any correlations embedded in the time series, which leads to an exponential distribution of the recurrence intervals (Bunde, Eichner, Havlin, & Kantelhardt, 2003, 2004).

In order to attack these problems, we can utilize the recurrence interval analysis, which has been applied to a variety of fields.

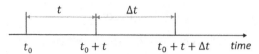

Figure 1.1 Schematic plot. A dragon king occurred at time t_0, and no dragon kings occurred between t_0 and the present time $t_0 + t$. The next dragon king might occur before time $t_0 + t + \Delta t$.

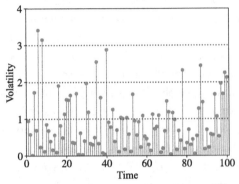

Figure 1.2 Illustration of recurrence intervals of a normalized volatility time series for $Q = 1, 2,$ and 3.

1.2 Defining Recurrence Intervals

In essence, recurrence intervals are the waiting times between successive events. Consider a segment of a normalized volatility time series $\{v(1), \cdots, v(T)\}$, as shown in Figure 1.2. For a given threshold Q that has the same units as v, we define events as volatilities that are greater than Q. Figure 1.2 shows three horizontal dotted lines corresponding to $Q = 1, 2,$ and 3. For $Q = 3$, we obtain two events, which define one recurrence interval $\{\tau_1\}$. For $Q = 2$, we obtain eight events, resulting in seven recurrence intervals $\{\tau_1, \cdots, \tau_7\}$. Note that, before defining events with Q, we usually standardize or normalize time series such that Q becomes dimensionless.

When the time series is sufficiently long, we have

$$T \approx \sum_{i=1}^{n} \tau_i, \tag{1.1}$$

and the mean recurrence interval is

$$\langle \tau \rangle \approx T/n, \tag{1.2}$$

where n is a decreasing function of Q. Hence, $\langle \tau \rangle$ is an increasing function of Q. We note that Eq. (1.1) and Eq. (1.2) do not hold when Q is too large (n is small).

There are other methods that can be used to define events. One natural way is to use quantiles. We can define events as those largest points with a percentage of Q. Podobnik, Horvatic, Petersen, and Stanley (2009) and Bogachev and Bunde (2009a) found that the mean recurrence interval $\langle \tau \rangle$ is related to the percentage Q of extremes:

$$\langle \tau \rangle = \frac{1}{\int_Q^{+\infty} p(x)\mathrm{d}x} = \frac{1}{1-Q}, \tag{1.3}$$

where x is a certain financial variable under investigation, $p(x)$ is its probability distribution, and

$$\int_{-\infty}^{z} p(x)\mathrm{d}x = 1 - Q = \frac{n}{T}. \tag{1.4}$$

When x is a financial return, z can be interpreted as the Value at Risk (VaR).

There are various names for "recurrence interval." Among them, "return interval" is often used in econophysics. However, "return" is a terminology in finance that refers to the percent of money made or lost on an investment over some period of time. Hence, in econophysics, we strongly suggest using "recurrence interval" instead of "return interval" to avoid any potential confusions.

1.3 Recurrence Interval Analysis

The two questions raised in Section 1.1 can be formulated based on the probability distribution of the recurrence intervals.

1.3.1 Hazard Probability

The probability $W(\Delta t|t)$ that the next dragon king might occur before time $t_0 + t + \Delta t$ is known as the hazard probability or hazard function. In order to estimate the empirical hazard function $W_{\mathrm{emp}}(\Delta t|t)$, we count the number $\#(\tau > t)$ of recurrence intervals with values greater than t and the number $\#(t < \tau \leq t + \Delta t)$ of recurrence intervals that fall within the range of $(t, t + \Delta t]$. We obtain that

$$W_{\mathrm{emp}}(\Delta t|t) = \frac{\#(t < \tau \leq t + \Delta t)}{\#(\tau > t)}. \tag{1.5}$$

Alternatively, when we obtain the recurrence distribution $p_Q(\tau; \Phi)$ in which Φ is the set of calibrated parameters of the distribution, the probability density function that we must wait an additional time Δt until the next event can be obtained by Bayes' theorem for conditional probabilities:

$$p_Q(\Delta t|t) = \frac{p_Q(t + \Delta t; \Phi)}{\int_t^{\infty} p_Q(t; \Phi)\mathrm{d}t}, \tag{1.6}$$

Hence, the hazard probability $W(\Delta t|t)$ can be formulated as follows (Bogachev, Eichner, & Bunde, 2007; Sornette & Knopoff, 1997):

$$
W(\Delta t|t) = \int_0^{\Delta t} p_Q(t'|t)dt' = \frac{\int_0^{\Delta t} p_Q(t + t'; \Phi)dt'}{\int_t^\infty p_Q(t; \Phi)dt}
$$

$$
= \frac{\int_t^{t+\Delta t} p_Q(u; \Phi)du}{\int_t^\infty p_Q(t; \Phi)dt}, \tag{1.7}
$$

where a change of variable $t + t' = u$ is used, and Φ is the set of the estimated parameters that may or may not depend on the threshold Q.

When Q is not too large, we can use Eq. (1.5) to calculate the hazard probabilities for different values of t and Δt. However, when Q is large, Eq. (1.5) becomes unsuitable since we only have very few recurrence intervals. It is also impossible to estimate the empirical distribution $p_{\mathrm{emp},Q}(t)$ and impossible to fit it with $p_Q(t; \Phi)$. The key idea of the recurrence interval analysis aims to solve this difficulty. In the same vein, we obtain the distributions $p_Q(t; \Phi)$ for relatively small thresholds Q and try to figure out what the relationship between Φ and Q is. If the distributions $p_Q(t; \Phi)$ for different thresholds Q have a scaling behavior, it is reasonable to conjecture that the distributions for large thresholds Q have the same parameter set Φ. Even if there is no scaling behavior in the recurrence interval distributions, we can still simply extrapolate to obtain Φ for large thresholds Q.

1.3.2 Expected Hazard Time

There is another expression related to the second question: "The longer it has been since the last extreme event, the longer the expected time till the next?" (Sornette & Knopoff, 1997). It concerns about the expected time until the next extreme event (Sornette & Knopoff, 1997). We call it "the expected residual time" or "the expected hazard time." The expected hazard time $\langle \Delta t \rangle$ can be estimated empirically when the threshold Q is not too large.

Alternatively, if we know the recurrence interval distribution $p_Q(t; \Phi)$, the expected residual time $\langle \Delta t \rangle$ is expressed as follows (Sornette & Knopoff, 1997):

$$
\langle \Delta t \rangle = \int_0^\infty t' p_Q(t'|t)dt' = \frac{\int_0^\infty t' p_Q(t + t'; \Phi)dt'}{\int_t^\infty p_Q(t; \Phi)dt}
$$

$$
= \frac{\int_t^\infty (u - t)p_Q(u; \Phi)du}{\int_t^\infty p_Q(t; \Phi)dt}, \tag{1.8}
$$

where a change of variable $t + t' = u$ is used. Again, we should aim to reveal the dependence of Φ on Q for small thresholds to conjecture the expected residual time for extreme events when the threshold Q is large.

2 Recurrence Interval Distributions

2.1 Empirical Distributions

We first obtain the recurrence interval time series $\{\tau(i) : i = 1, \cdots, N\}$ for different thresholds Q. In order to determine the empirical distribution for a recurrence interval time series, we adopt the logarithmic binning. The sizes of the bins are logarithmically spaced in $[1, \max_{i \in \{1,\cdots,N\}} \{\tau(i)\}]$. Since recurrence intervals are integers, the duplicate integers of the rounded edges are discarded and the remaining rounded edges form a sequence b_j. For the edges except 1 and $\max_{i \in \{1,\cdots,N\}} \{\tau(i)\}$, we add 0.5 to them and form the final bins $\{e_j\}$. On each bin $(e_i, e_{i+1}]$, the empirical probability density can be calculated by

$$P_Q \left(\tau = \frac{e_i + e_{i+1}}{2} \right) = \frac{\#(e_i < \tau \le e_{i+1})}{N(e_{i+1} - e_i)}, \tag{2.1}$$

where $\#()$ denotes the number of recurrence intervals that satisfies the condition in the parentheses.

2.2 Candidate Distributions

The determination of an analytic distribution is at the core of recurrence interval analysis. If $p(\tau)$ is an analytic expression of the probability density of recurrence intervals, we have the following two equations:

$$\int_0^\infty p(\tau)\mathrm{d}\tau = 1 \tag{2.2}$$

and

$$\int_0^\infty \tau p(\tau)\mathrm{d}\tau = \langle \tau \rangle. \tag{2.3}$$

which allow us to reduce the number of parameters in the fits. Note that we have dropped Q from p and $\langle \tau \rangle$ for brevity.

2.2.1 Exponential Distribution

For uncorrelated time series, we have

$$p_{\mathrm{Exp}}(\tau) = \frac{1}{\langle \tau \rangle} \exp \left[-\frac{\tau}{\langle \tau \rangle} \right]. \tag{2.4}$$

This distribution is universal since $f(\tau/\langle \tau \rangle) = p_{\mathrm{Exp}}(\tau)\langle \tau \rangle$ does not have any parameters and shows a scaling behavior.

2.2.2 Power-law Distribution

For strong nonlinear correlated time series or multifractal time series, Bogachev et al. (2007) found that the recurrence intervals may be distributed as a power law:

$$p_{PL}(\tau) = \frac{A}{\langle \tau \rangle} \left(\frac{\tau}{\langle \tau \rangle} \right)^{-\alpha - 1}, \tag{2.5}$$

where the power-law exponent $\alpha > 0$ depends on Q or the average recurrence interval $\langle \tau \rangle$. Using Eq. (2.2), we obtain that

$$A = \alpha. \tag{2.6}$$

2.2.3 Power-law Distribution with an Exponential Cutoff

The power-law distribution with an exponential cutoff can be expressed as follows:

$$p_{PLExp}(\tau) = c\tau^{-\beta - 1} \exp(-k\tau). \tag{2.7}$$

Using Eq. (2.2) and Eq. (2.3), we obtain that

$$k = \frac{\Gamma(-\beta + 1)}{\Gamma(-\beta)} \frac{1}{\langle \tau \rangle}, \tag{2.8}$$

and

$$c = \frac{\langle \tau \rangle^{\beta} \Gamma(-\beta)^{\beta - 1}}{\Gamma(-\beta + 1)^{\beta}}. \tag{2.9}$$

where $\Gamma(x)$ has the form of Gamma functions, but is not a Gamma function.

2.2.4 Double Power-law Distribution

The double power-law distribution can be expressed as follows:

$$\langle \tau \rangle P_{DPL}(\tau) \sim \begin{cases} A_1 \left(\frac{\tau}{\langle \tau \rangle} \right)^{-\alpha_1 - 1} & \text{if } 1 < \tau < \tau_c \\ A_2 \left(\frac{\tau}{\langle \tau \rangle} \right)^{-\alpha_2 - 1} & \text{if } \tau > \tau_c \end{cases}, \tag{2.10}$$

where A_1, A_2, α_1, and α_2 are parameters that can be estimated by regression. The double power-law distribution was observed in the recurrence intervals of energy dissipation rate in three-dimensional fully developed turbulence (Liu, Jiang, Ren, & Zhou, 2009).

2.2.5 q-exponential Distribution

The q-exponential distribution can be expressed as follows:

$$p_{qExp}(\tau) = (2 - q)\lambda[1 + (q - 1)\lambda\tau]^{-\frac{1}{q-1}}, \tag{2.11}$$

The expectation of τ from the q-exponential distribution is $1/[\lambda(3 - 2q)]$. To ensure the existence of $\langle\tau\rangle$, q must be less than $3/2$. The parameter λ can be expressed using q and $\langle\tau\rangle$:

$$\lambda = \frac{1}{\langle\tau\rangle(3 - 2q)}. \tag{2.12}$$

2.2.6 Weibull Distribution

The Weibull distribution can be expressed as follows:

$$p_{\text{WBL}}(\tau) = \frac{\zeta}{d}\left(\frac{\tau}{d}\right)^{\zeta-1}\exp\left[-\left(\frac{\tau}{d}\right)^{\zeta}\right]. \tag{2.13}$$

The expectation of the recurrence intervals is $d \cdot \Gamma(1 + 1/\zeta)$. Hence, the parameter d can be expressed in terms of ζ and $\langle\tau\rangle$ (Jiang, Canabarro, Podobnik, Stanley, & Zhou, 2016):

$$d = \frac{\langle\tau\rangle}{\Gamma\left(1 + \frac{1}{\zeta}\right)}. \tag{2.14}$$

2.2.7 Stretched Exponential Distribution

The stretched exponential distribution can be expressed as follows:

$$p_{\text{StrExp}}(\tau) = a\exp[-(b\tau)^{\gamma}], \tag{2.15}$$

Inserting the stretched exponential function of Eq. (2.15) into Eq. (2.2), we obtain

$$\frac{a}{\gamma b}\Gamma\left(\frac{1}{\gamma}\right) = 1, \tag{2.16}$$

where $\Gamma(x)$ is the Gamma function. Inserting the stretched exponential function of Eq. (2.15) into Eq. (2.3), we obtain that

$$\frac{a}{\gamma b^2}\Gamma\left(\frac{2}{\gamma}\right) = \langle\tau\rangle. \tag{2.17}$$

By solving Eqs. (2.16) and (2.17) and using γ and $\langle\tau\rangle$ for the stretched exponential distribution, we obtain that

$$a = \frac{\gamma\Gamma(2/\gamma)}{\Gamma(1/\gamma)^2\langle\tau\rangle} \tag{2.18}$$

and

$$b = \frac{\Gamma(2/\gamma)}{\Gamma(1/\gamma)\langle\tau\rangle}. \tag{2.19}$$

2.2.8 Stretched Weibull Distribution

Alternatively, one can write a formula similar to the Weibull distribution that is called the stretched Weibull distribution (Bogachev & Bunde, 2009b; Bunde et al., 2012):

$$p_{\text{StrWBL}}(\tau) = \frac{C}{\langle \tau \rangle} \left(\frac{\tau}{\langle \tau \rangle} \right)^{\mu-1} \exp \left[-b \left(\frac{\tau}{\langle \tau \rangle} \right)^{\mu} \right]. \tag{2.20}$$

2.3 Fitting Procedure

2.3.1 Ordinary Least Squares Regression

When a nonexponential distribution function $p(\tau; \Phi)$ described in Section 2.2 is adopted to fit an empirical recurrence interval distribution $p_{\text{Emp}}(\tau)$, one can use the ordinary least squares (OLS) regression, which is to minimize the following objective function:

$$O(\Phi) = \sum \left[p(\tau; \Phi) - p_{\text{Emp}}(\tau) \right]^2, \tag{2.21}$$

where $\Phi = \{\phi_1, \cdots, \phi_m\}$ is the set of parameters. The equation

$$\hat{\Phi} = \arg\min_{\Phi} O(\Phi) \tag{2.22}$$

can be solved analytically or numerically, due to the form of the probability function.

2.3.2 Maximum Likelihood Estimation

Alternatively, we can utilize maximum likelihood estimation (MLE) to estimate the distributional parameters. The likelihood function of probability function $p(\tau; \Phi)$ is

$$L(\Phi) = \prod_{i=1}^{n} p(\tau_i; \Phi). \tag{2.23}$$

In order to implement the method of maximum likelihood, we need to find the parameters Φ that maximizes the likelihood $L(\Phi)$:

$$\hat{\Phi} = \arg\min_{\Phi} L(\Phi). \tag{2.24}$$

Equivalently, we can maximize the natural logarithm of the likelihood function:

$$\hat{\Phi} = \arg\min_{\Phi} \ln L(\Phi) = \arg\min_{\Phi} \sum_{i=1}^{n} \ln p(\tau_i; \Phi). \tag{2.25}$$

Taking the derivative of the logarithmic likelihood function and setting it to 0, we obtain:

$$\frac{\partial \log L(\Phi)}{\partial \phi_i} = 0 \tag{2.26}$$

for $i = 1, \cdots, m$. Solving Eq. (2.26) analytically or numerically, we obtain the estimation of Φ.

2.3.3 Logarithmic Likelihood Functions

The logarithmic likelihood function of the power-law distribution expressed in Eq. (2.5) is

$$\ln L_{PL} = n \ln \alpha + n\alpha \ln \langle \tau \rangle - (\alpha + 1) \sum_{i=1}^{n} \ln \tau_i. \tag{2.27}$$

We obtain that

$$\frac{d \ln L_{PL}}{d\alpha} = \frac{n}{\alpha} + n \ln \langle \tau \rangle - \sum_{i=1}^{n} \ln \tau_i = 0. \tag{2.28}$$

It follows that

$$\alpha = n \left[\sum_{i=1}^{n} \ln \frac{\tau_i}{\langle \tau \rangle} \right]^{-1}, \tag{2.29}$$

which is known as the Hill estimator (Clauset et al., 2009; Hill, 1975).

The logarithmic likelihood function of the power-law distribution with an exponential cutoff expressed in Eq. (2.7) is

$$\ln L_{PLExp} = n \ln c - (\beta + 1) \sum_{i=1}^{n} \ln \tau_i - k \sum_{i=1}^{n} \tau_i, \tag{2.30}$$

where c and k are functions of β.

The logarithmic likelihood function of the double power-law distribution expressed in Eq. (2.10) is

$$\ln L_{DPL} = \sum_{i=1}^{n} \ln A_j + \ln \langle \tau \rangle \sum_{i=1}^{n} \alpha_j - \sum_{i=1}^{n} (\alpha_j + 1) \ln \tau_i, \tag{2.31}$$

where $j = 1$ if $1 < \tau < \tau_c$ and $j = 2$ if $\tau > \tau_c$.

The logarithmic likelihood function of the stretched exponential distribution expressed in Eq. (2.15) is

$$\ln L_{StrExp} = n \ln a - \sum_{i=1}^{n} (b\tau_i)^{\gamma}, \tag{2.32}$$

The logarithmic likelihood function of the q-exponential distribution expressed in Eq. (2.11) is

$$\ln L_{qE} = n\ln[\lambda(2-q)] - \frac{1}{q-1}\sum_{i=1}^{n}\ln[1+(q-1)\lambda\tau_i]. \tag{2.33}$$

Most of the relevant formulas for the estimation of stretched exponential distributions can be found in (Sornette, 2004, Chap. 6). In addition, Malevergne and Sornette (2006, Chap. 2) derived that the power law is asymptotically nested in the stretched exponential family, which allows the rigorous use of the log-likelihood ratio Wilks test.

The logarithmic likelihood function of the Weibull distribution expressed in Eq. (2.13) is

$$\ln L_{WBL} = n\ln\frac{\alpha}{\beta} + \sum_{i=1}^{n}\left[(\alpha-1)\ln\frac{\tau_i}{\beta} - \left(\frac{\tau_i}{\beta}\right)^{\alpha}\right], \tag{2.34}$$

in which n is the number of recurrence intervals.

The logarithmic likelihood function of the stretched Weibull distribution in Eq. (2.20) is

$$\ln L_{StrWBL} = n\ln c - (\delta+1)\sum_{i=1}^{n}\ln\tau_i - k\sum_{i=1}^{n}\tau_i. \tag{2.35}$$

2.4 Goodness-of-fit

Here, we focus on quantifying the goodness-of-fit of a pre-chosen distribution to the empirical sample. When there are more than one candidate distributions, the Wilks' test can be adopted for pairwise comparison (Malevergne et al., 2005; Malevergne & Sornette, 2006).

2.4.1 Statistical Tests Through Bootstrapping

In order to quantify the goodness-of-fit of the estimated probability distribution function $p(\tau;\hat{\Phi})$, we can perform statistical tests. The idea is to check how likely the sample is drawn from the fitted distribution $p(\tau;\hat{\Phi})$. The null hypothesis H_0 and the alternative hypothesis H_1 are the following:

H_0: The sample comes from $p(\tau;\hat{\Phi})$;
H_1: The sample does not come from $p(\tau;\hat{\Phi})$.

We need to define a statistic $D(F_{emp}(\tau), F(\tau;\hat{\Phi}))$ that measures the distance between the empirical cumulative distribution function $F_{emp}(\tau)$ and the fitted cumulative distribution function $F(\tau; \hat{\Phi})$. The D value for the real realization of the recurrence interval can be expressed as follows:

$$D_{\text{emp}} = D(F_{\text{emp}}(\tau), F(\tau; \hat{\Phi})). \tag{2.36}$$

Different definitions of $D(F_{\text{emp}}(\tau), F(\tau; \hat{\Phi}))$ result in different statistical tests.

In order to test the hypothesis that the empirical cumulative distribution function $F_{\text{emp}}(\tau)$ can be well fitted by the cumulative distribution function $F(\tau; \hat{\Phi})$, we adopt the bootstrap method (Clauset et al., 2009; González et al., 2008). We generate many (say, one thousand) synthetic samples from the cumulative distribution function $F(\tau; \hat{\Phi})$ (Press, Teukolsky, Vetterling, & Flannery, 1996). For each synthetic sample, a distance is obtained as follows:

$$D_{\text{sim}} = D(F_{\text{sim,emp}}(\tau), F_{\text{sim}}(\tau; \hat{\Phi})), \tag{2.37}$$

where $F_{\text{sim, emp}}(\tau)$ is the empirical cumulative distribution function of the synthetic sample, and $F_{\text{sim}}(\tau; \hat{\Phi})$ is the fitted cumulative distribution function of the synthetic sample.

We then obtain an empirical distribution $p(D_{\text{sim}})$ of D_{sim}, as illustrated in Figure 2.1. The probability that the null hypothesis H_0 holds is defined as the fraction of D_{sim} values that are greater than D:

$$p\text{-value} = \int_D^\infty p(D_{\text{sim}}) \mathrm{d}D_{\text{sim}}. \tag{2.38}$$

Someone may be confused by the meaning of the p-value. Here, a smaller value of D indicates a higher goodness-of-fit, which corresponds to a higher p-value.

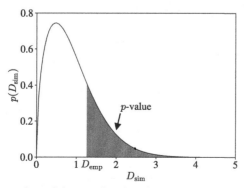

Figure 2.1 Illustration of the p-value that the null hypothesis H_0 holds based on the empirical distribution $p(D_{\text{sim}})$ of D_{sim}, where D is the distance value of the observed sample, while D_{sim} is the variable representing the distances from the synthetic samples.

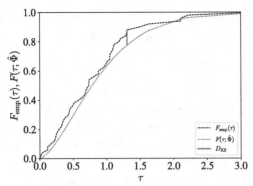

Figure 2.2 Definition of Kolmogorov–Smirnov (KS) statistic D_{KS}. The KS statistic is the largest difference between the empirical cumulative distribution function $F_{emp}(\tau)$ and the fitted cumulative distribution function $F(\tau; \hat{\Phi})$, shown as a vertical line segment (red online).

2.4.2 Kolmogorov–Smirnov Test

The one-sample Kolmogorov–Smirnov (KS) test is a widely used method. The one-sample KS statistic is defined as

$$D_{KS} = \max\left(\left|F_{emp}(\tau) - F(\tau; \hat{\Phi})\right|\right), \tag{2.39}$$

which quantifies the maximum distance between the empirical cumulative distribution function $F_{emp}(\tau)$ and the fitted cumulative distribution function $F(\tau; \hat{\Phi})$, as shown in Figure 2.2. If there is a lower bound τ_{min}, the KS statistic becomes

$$D_{KS} = \max_{\tau \geq \tau_{min}}\left(\left|F_{emp}(\tau) - F(\tau; \hat{\Phi})\right|\right). \tag{2.40}$$

For each synthetic sample, the value of the KS statistic is obtained as follows:

$$D_{KS,sim} = \max\left(\left|F_{sim, emp}(\tau) - F_{sim}(\tau; \hat{\Phi})\right|\right), \tag{2.41}$$

where $F_{sim, emp}(\tau)$ is the empirical cumulative distribution function of the synthetic sample and $F_{sim}(\tau; \hat{\Phi})$ is the fitted cumulative distribution function of the synthetic sample.

Kolmogorov (1933) proved that the limiting distribution $p(K_n)$ of the variable

$$K_n = \sqrt{n}D, \tag{2.42}$$

where n is the number of data points.

$$\lim_{n \to \infty} \Pr\{K_n' < K_n\} = F(K_n) = 1 - 2\sum_{j=1}^{\infty}(-1)^{j-1}\exp\left(-2nj^2 D_{KS}^2\right). \tag{2.43}$$

or equivalently

$$\lim_{n\to\infty} \Pr\{K'_n < K_n\} = F(K_n) = \frac{\sqrt{2\pi}}{\sqrt{n}D_{\text{KS}}} \sum_{j=1}^{\infty} \exp\left(-\frac{(2j-1)^2\pi^2}{8nD_{\text{KS}}^2}\right). \tag{2.44}$$

Smirnov (1939) provided a simpler proof of the limiting distribution.

2.4.3 Cramér-von Mises Test

The Cramér-von Mises (CvM) statistic has also been utilized in the investigation of recurrence interval distributions. The CvM statistic is defined as follows (Pearson & Stephens, 1962; Stephens, 1964, 1970):

$$W_n^2 = n \int_{-\infty}^{\infty} \left[F_{\text{emp}}(\tau) - F(\tau; \hat{\Phi})\right]^2 dF(\tau; \hat{\Phi}), \tag{2.45}$$

where n is the number of recurrence intervals. For synthetic samples, we have

$$W_{n,\text{sim}}^2 = n \int_{-\infty}^{\infty} \left[F_{\text{sim,emp}}(\tau) - F_{\text{sim}}(\tau; \hat{\Phi})\right]^2 dF_{\text{sim}}(\tau; \hat{\Phi}). \tag{2.46}$$

One can also introduce a weight function $\psi\left[F(\tau; \hat{\Phi})\right]$ into W_n^2 as for D_{KS} (Anderson & Darling, 1952). For a sequence of recurrence intervals $\tau_1, \cdots, \tau_n$ that have been sorted in ascending order, the computational form of the W_n^2 statistic is given by (Stephens, 1970, 1974)

$$W_n^2 = \frac{1}{12n} + \sum_{i=1}^{n} \left(F_{\text{emp}}(\tau_i) - \frac{2i-1}{2n}\right)^2. \tag{2.47}$$

Anderson and Darling (1952) derived the limiting distribution of W_n^2:

$$F_{\text{CvM}}(x) = \lim_{n\to\infty} \Pr(W_n^2 \le x) = \frac{1}{\pi\sqrt{x}} \sum_{j=0}^{\infty} (-1)^j \binom{-\frac{1}{2}}{j} \tag{2.48}$$

$$.(4j+1)^{\frac{1}{2}} \exp\left(-\frac{(4j+1)^2)}{16x}\right) K_{\frac{1}{4}}\left(\frac{(4j+1)^2)}{16x}\right), \tag{2.49}$$

where $K_{\frac{1}{4}}(x)$ is the standard Bessel function and

$$\binom{-\frac{1}{2}}{j} = (-1)^j \frac{\Gamma(j+\frac{1}{2})}{\Gamma(\frac{1}{2})j!}. \tag{2.50}$$

According to Stephens (1970), the p-value can be approximated by

$$p\text{-value} = 0.05\exp(2.79 - 6T^*), \tag{2.51}$$

where

$$T^* = \frac{W^2 - 0.4/n - 0.6/n^2}{1.0 + 1.0/n} \tag{2.52}$$

and the critical value C_α is $C_\alpha = 0.284$ for $\alpha = 15\%$, $C_\alpha = 0.347$ for $\alpha = 10\%$, $C_\alpha = 0.461$ for $\alpha = 5\%$, $C_\alpha = 0.581$ for $\alpha = 2.5\%$, and $C_\alpha = 0.743$ for $\alpha = 1.0\%$. When n is large enough, we have $T^* \approx W^2$.

2.4.4 Weighted Kolmogorov–Smirnov Test

As pointed out by Press et al. (2007), the KS test tends to be more sensitive around the median value of the probability function ($p(\tau) = 0.5$) and less sensitive at the ends of the distribution ($p(\tau)$ is close to 0 or 1). Hence, several other measures for goodness-of-fit have been proposed.

Anderson and Darling (1952) introduced a weighted KS statistic, which is defined as follows:

$$D_{\text{KSW}} = \max \left| F_{\text{emp}}(\tau) - F(\tau; \hat{\Phi}) \right| \sqrt{\psi \left[F(\tau; \hat{\Phi}) \right]}, \tag{2.53}$$

where ψ is the weight function. When $\psi \left[F(\tau; \hat{\Phi}) \right] = 1$, D_{KSW} becomes the KS statistic D_{KS}. When the weight function is

$$\psi \left[F(\tau; \hat{\Phi}) \right] = \frac{1}{F(\tau; \hat{\Phi})(1 - F(\tau; \hat{\Phi}))}, \tag{2.54}$$

we obtain the Anderson-Darling (AD) statistic

$$D_{\text{AD}} = \max \frac{\left| F_{\text{emp}}(\tau) - F(\tau; \hat{\Phi}) \right|}{\sqrt{F(\tau; \hat{\Phi})(1 - F(\tau; \hat{\Phi}))}}. \tag{2.55}$$

This KSW (or AD) statistic puts higher weight on the middle part of the cumulative distributions. For the two weight functions mentioned above, Anderson and Darling (1952) derived the explicit limiting distributions of D_{KS} and $\sqrt{n} D_{\text{AD}}$.

The values of the AD statistic for the synthetic samples can thus be calculated by

$$D_{\text{AD, sim}} = \max \frac{\left| F_{\text{sim, emp}}(\tau) - F_{\text{sim}}(\tau; \hat{\Phi}) \right|}{\sqrt{F_{\text{sim}}(\tau; \hat{\Phi})(1 - F_{\text{sim}}(\tau; \hat{\Phi}))}}. \tag{2.56}$$

One can use $D_{\text{AD, sim}}$ or $D_{\text{KSW, sim}}$ equivalently.

2.5 Scaling and Multiscaling Behavior

An important question is whether there is a scaling behavior in the recurrence interval distributions $P_q(\tau)$ for different thresholds Q. To attack this problem, one considers the scaled distributions:

$$p_Q(\tau) = \frac{1}{\langle \tau \rangle} f_Q \left(\frac{\tau}{\langle \tau \rangle} \right). \tag{2.57}$$

The scaling behavior exists if f_Q is independent of the threshold Q:

$$f_Q\left(\frac{\tau}{\langle\tau\rangle}\right) = f\left(\frac{\tau}{\langle\tau\rangle}\right). \tag{2.58}$$

There are a few methods that can be adopted to check if there is a scaling behavior.

2.5.1 Statistical Tests

Assume that we investigate a set of m thresholds, $\mathbf{Q} = \{Q_1, \cdots, Q_m\}$, and obtain m recurrence interval time series $\{\{\tau_{Q,1}, \cdots, \tau_{Q,n_i}\} : i = 1, \cdots, m\}$. Then, to test Eq. (2.58) is equivalent to test the following:

$$f_{Q_1}\left(\frac{\tau}{\langle\tau\rangle}\right) = \cdots = f_{Q_m}\left(\frac{\tau}{\langle\tau\rangle}\right). \tag{2.59}$$

Consider two scaled distributions f_{Q_i} and f_{Q_j}, where $Q_1 \neq Q_2$, $Q_i \in \mathbf{Q}$, and $Q_j \in \mathbf{Q}$. The null hypothesis H_0 and the alternative hypothesis H_1 are the following:

H_0: $f_{Q_i} = f_{Q_j}$;
H_1: $f_{Q_i} \neq f_{Q_j}$.

In the literature, most studies test all the $m(m-1)/2$ pairs of Q_i and Q_j. However, it is actually sufficient to accept or reject the null hypothesis by testing only for the (Q_1, Q_m) pair since the distance between $f(Q_1)$ and $f(Q_m)$ is the largest.

There are also quite a few methods that can be used to test if two empirical distributions are different or not (Clauset et al., 2009; González et al., 2008). Here, we consider defining a statistic $D(F_{Q_i}, F_{Q_j})$ that measures the distance between the two empirical cumulative distribution functions F_{Q_i} and F_{Q_j}. Different definitions of $D(F_{Q_i}, F_{Q_j})$ result in different statistical tests. If the distribution $p(D)$ of D is known, the p-value can be obtained as follows:

$$p\text{-value} = \int_D^\infty p(D')\mathrm{d}D', \tag{2.60}$$

which is the probability that the null hypothesis H_0 holds.

For the two-sample KS test, Smirnov (1939) considered the random variable

$$K_{n_i n_j} = \sqrt{N_e}D, \tag{2.61}$$

where

$$N_e = \frac{n_i n_j}{n_i + n_j} \tag{2.62}$$

is the effective number, and n_i and n_j are respectively the numbers of recurrence intervals corresponding to Q_i and Q_j, and proved that the limiting distribution of $K_{n_i n_j}$ is

$$F_{KS}(K_{n_i n_j}) = 1 - 2 \sum_{j=1}^{\infty} (-1)^{j-1} \exp\left(-2N_e j^2 D_{KS}^2\right).$$ (2.63)

Stephens (1970) gave an approximate expression of the p-value:

$$p\text{-value} = 1 - F_{KS}\left(\left[\sqrt{N_e} + 0.12 + 0.11/\sqrt{N_e}\right] D\right),$$ (2.64)

The critical value at the significance level α is (Stephens, 1974)

$$CV = \frac{C_\alpha}{\sqrt{N_e}},$$ (2.65)

where $C_\alpha = 1.138$ for $\alpha = 15\%$, $C_\alpha = 1.224$ for $\alpha = 10\%$, $C_\alpha = 1.358$ for $\alpha = 5\%$, $C_\alpha = 1.480$ for $\alpha = 2.5\%$, and $C_\alpha = 1.628$ for $\alpha = 1.0\%$.

2.5.2 Moments

Wang et al. (2008) suggested that the detection of multiscaling can be done by investigating the dependence of the moments of recurrence intervals on the threshold. In other words, the distributions of recurrence intervals may exhibit multiscaling behavior if the moments show a systematic tendency with the threshold Q. The moments $(Z_m)^m$ of the scaled recurrence intervals $x = \tau/\langle\tau\rangle$ for a given Q are defined as follows:

$$Z_m = \left\langle\left(\frac{\tau}{\langle\tau\rangle}\right)^m\right\rangle^{\frac{1}{m}} = \left[\int_0^\infty x^m f_Q(x) dx\right]^{\frac{1}{m}}.$$ (2.66)

where the mean interval $\langle\tau\rangle$ depends on the threshold Q. When $m = 1$, by definition, we have

$$Z_1 = \int_0^\infty \frac{\tau}{\langle\tau\rangle} f_Q\left(\frac{\tau}{\langle\tau\rangle}\right) d\frac{\tau}{\langle\tau\rangle} = \int_0^\infty \frac{\tau}{\langle\tau\rangle} p_Q(\tau) d\tau = 1,$$ (2.67)

which is independent of Q. If there is a scaling behavior such that $f_Q(x) = f(x)$, we have

$$Z_m = \left[\int_0^\infty x^m f(x) dx\right]^{\frac{1}{m}},$$ (2.68)

which is a univariate function of the order m and is independent of any other variables including the threshold q and the mean recurrence interval $\langle\tau\rangle$. On the contrary, if there is a multiscaling behavior, the m-th moment Z_m is not constant and is dependent of Q or $\langle\tau\rangle$ for all $m \neq 1$.

Empirical studies show that (Ren & Zhou, 2008; Wang et al., 2008), if multi-scaling exists, Z_m is a decreasing function of $\langle \tau \rangle$ when $m < 1$ and an increasing function of $\langle \tau \rangle$ when $m > 1$ but not too large. Furthermore, the moment curves may show a power-law-like form with respect to $\langle \tau \rangle$:

$$Z_m \sim \langle \tau \rangle^{\kappa_m}. \tag{2.69}$$

We note that $\kappa_1 \equiv 0$. In addition, $\kappa_m < 0$ when $m < 1$ and $\kappa_m > 0$ when $m > 1$. If $\langle \tau \rangle \sim Q^\beta$, we have

$$Z_m \sim Q^{\kappa_m \beta}. \tag{2.70}$$

If the recurrence interval distributions exhibit a scaling behavior, Z_m is independent of $\langle \tau \rangle$ and Q such that the exponents κ_m and $\kappa_m \beta$ is close to 0. An exponent κ_m (or $\kappa_m \beta$) that is significantly different from 0 implies that there is a multiscaling behavior.

Ren and Zhou (2008) performed an interesting extended self-similarity (ESS) analysis relating two moments of orders m_1 and m_2 as introduced by Benzi et al. (1993). According to Eq. (2.69), we have

$$(Z_{m_1})^{m_1} \sim (Z_{m_2})^{m_2 \xi(m,n)}. \tag{2.71}$$

We denote that

$$Z_{m_1,m_2} = \frac{Z_{m_1}}{Z_{m_2}}. \tag{2.72}$$

If Z_{m_1,m_2} scales with respect to Z_{m_2} as

$$Z_{m_1,m_2} \sim \left(Z_{m_2}\right)^\alpha \tag{2.73}$$

together with Eq. (2.71), we have

$$(\alpha + 1)/m_1 = \xi(m_1,m_2)/m_2. \tag{2.74}$$

If the recurrence interval distribution can be scaled as follows:

$$p_Q(\tau) = \frac{1}{Z_{m_2}} f\left(\frac{\tau}{Z_{m_2}}\right), \tag{2.75}$$

we obtain that

$$\xi(m_1,m_2) = m_1/m_2. \tag{2.76}$$

In this case, we have

$$\alpha = 0. \tag{2.77}$$

In other words, $Z_{m,n}$ is independent of Z_{m_2}. Fixing $m_2 = 1$ and rewriting $m_1 = m$, we obtain from Eq. (2.74) that

$$\alpha(m) = \xi(m,1)/m - 1. \tag{2.78}$$

Since $\xi(1,1) = 1$, we have $\alpha(1) = 0$ when $m = 1$. This ESS framework was also used to investigate scaling behaviors in the exit times in turbulence (Zhou, Sornette, & Yuan, 2006) and intertrade durations (Eisler & Kertész, 2006).

If we know the distribution $p_Q(\tau)$, we can obtain Z_m analytically or numerically. For the stretched exponential distribution expressed in Eq. (2.15), we have (Wang et al., 2008)

$$Z_m = \frac{1}{a}\left[\frac{\Gamma((m+1)/\gamma)}{\Gamma(1/\gamma)}\right]^{1/m}. \tag{2.79}$$

We can thus investigate Z_m with respect to m for observed samples.

3 Memory Effects

3.1 Short Memory

In order to investigate the presence of short-term correlations in the recurrence interval time series, we often check the statistical properties of a few successive recurrence intervals and compare them with those of random time series (i.e., shuffle recurrence interval time series). There are three ways that are often adopted to quantify the short-term memory in the recurrence interval time series.

3.1.1 Conditional Recurrence Interval Distributions

The conditional distribution $p_Q(\tau|\tau_0)$ computes the probability of finding a recurrence interval τ immediately following a recurrence interval τ_0 (Livina, Havlin, & Bunde, 2005; Livina, Tuzov, Havlin, & Bunde, 2005; Yamasaki, Muchnik, Havlin, Bunde, & Stanley, 2005). Since the size of a recurrence interval time series is $1/\langle\tau\rangle$ of the size of the raw time series, it is not suitable to calculate $p_Q(\tau|\tau_0)$ for specific values of τ_0 for recurrence intervals with large Q or for short raw time series. Instead, in order to get better statistics, we perform this analysis at an aggregated level by looking at a range of τ_0 values. For this purpose, we sort the set of recurrence intervals in increasing order and divide it into m subsets, $B_{0,1}, \cdots, B_{0,m}$, such that each subset contains $\frac{1}{m}$ of the total number of recurrence intervals. For each recurrence interval τ_0 in $B_{0,i}$, we collect its successive recurrence interval τ and finally we obtain a set $B_i(\tau_0)$. For each $B_{0,i}$, we obtain an empirical distribution $p_Q(\tau|\tau_0)$.

For a time series without any correlations, the extracted recurrence interval time series above any threshold Q does not have any correlations. In this case, the conditional distribution $p_Q(\tau|\tau_0)$ does not depend on τ_0 and is identical to $p_Q(\tau)$ that is an exponential distribution. In addition, the scaled conditional distributions $\langle\tau|\tau_0\rangle p_Q(\tau|\tau_0)$ for different thresholds Q collapse onto a single curve with respect to the scaled recurrence interval $\tau/\langle\tau|\tau_0\rangle$, where $\langle\tau|\tau_0\rangle = \langle\tau\rangle$.

Since the average recurrence intervals in different $B_{0,i}$ are different, we again consider the scaled conditional distribution $\langle\tau|\tau_0\rangle p_Q(\tau|\tau_0)$. If there is short-term memory, we would expect that the m scaled conditional distributions do not collapse onto a single curve, which can be best illustrated by comparing the scaled conditional distributions for $B_{0,1}$ and $B_{0,m}$. For small $\tau/\langle\tau|\tau_0\rangle$, $\langle\tau|\tau_0\rangle p_Q(\tau|\tau_0)$ with τ_0 in $B_{0,1}$ is larger than that with τ_0 in $B_{0,m}$, while $\langle\tau|\tau_0\rangle p_Q(\tau|\tau_0)$ with τ_0 in $B_{0,m}$ shows values larger than that with τ_0 in $B_{0,1}$ when $\tau/\langle\tau|\tau_0\rangle$ is large. This means that small τ_0 tends to be followed by small τ and large τ_0 tends to be followed by large τ, which provides a piece of evidence for the presence of short-term memory.

3.1.2 Mean Conditional Recurrence Interval

In order to detect the possible presence of short-term memory in the recurrence interval time series, we can also resort to the mean conditional recurrence interval $\langle\tau|\tau_0\rangle$, which is the mean of those return intervals that immediately follow τ_0 (Livina, Havlin, et al., 2005; Livina, Tuzov, et al. 2005; Yamasaki et al. 2005). The set of recurrence intervals can also be divided into m subsets, $B_{0,1}, \cdots, B_{0,m}$. Here, we can take a much larger value of m in the calculation of the mean conditional recurrence intervals $\langle\tau|\tau_0\rangle$ than in the determination of the conditional distributions $p_Q(\tau|\tau_0)$.

For a recurrence interval time series that does not contain short memory, the mean conditional recurrence interval $\langle\tau|\tau_0\rangle$ does not depend on τ_0 such that

$$\langle\tau|\tau_0\rangle = \langle\tau\rangle. \tag{3.1}$$

Hence, the scaled mean conditional recurrence intervals $\langle\tau|\tau_0\rangle/\langle\tau\rangle = 1$ for all τ_0 values.

If there is short-term memory in the recurrence interval time series, the scaled mean conditional recurrence intervals $\langle\tau|\tau_0\rangle/\langle\tau\rangle$ deviate from 1. We usually plot the scaled mean conditional recurrence interval $\langle\tau|\tau_0\rangle/\langle\tau\rangle$ with respect to the scaled preceding interval $\tau_0/\langle\tau\rangle$. Empirical studies showed that $\langle\tau|\tau_0\rangle/\langle\tau\rangle$ strongly fluctuates in the whole region of $\tau_0/\langle\tau\rangle$, and approximately shows a monotonic increasing tendency as the increase of $\tau_0/\langle\tau\rangle$. This deviation indicates that for small (or large) preceding interval τ_0 the mean value of the following interval is also small (or large), which indicates the presence of short-term memory in the recurrence interval time series.

In addition, based on empirical studies, Wang et al. (2007) observed the following power-law relation:

$$\frac{\langle \tau | \tau_0 \rangle}{\langle \tau \rangle} = A \left(\frac{\tau_0}{\langle \tau \rangle} \right)^{\nu}, \tag{3.2}$$

while Ren and Zhou (2010) found a slightly modified power law in the following form:

$$\frac{\langle \tau | \tau_0 \rangle}{\langle \tau \rangle} = \left[1 + \mu \left(\frac{\tau_0}{\langle \tau \rangle} \right)^{-\gamma} \right] \left(\frac{\tau_0}{\langle \tau \rangle} \right)^{\nu}. \tag{3.3}$$

Such an explicit expression can be used to derive analytical expressions for risk measures.

3.2 Long Memory

Long memory is also called long-term memory, long-range dependence, long-term correlation, and long-range correlation. There are various methods that can be utilized to estimate the intensity of long memory (Jiang et al., 2019; Shao et al., 2012; Taqqu et al., 1995). The basic quantity for determining memory effects is the autocorrelation function (Bunde & Lennartz, 2012; Lennartz et al., 2008). Here, we briefly describe several other methods.

3.2.1 Rescaled Range Analysis

The rescaled range analysis (also referred as R/S analysis or Hurst analysis) is well known as a classic approach for the detection of long-range correlations in time series, which was invented by Hurst (1951) to analyze long-term variation of water level in hydrology. The method was then be studied mathematically by Mandelbrot and Wallis (1969a, 1969b) for fractional Brownian motions.

Consider a sub-series $\{y_i : i = 1, \cdots, s\}$ taken from the recurrence interval time series $\{\tau_i : i = 1, \cdots, n\}$. The cumulative profile of $\{y_i\}$ is

$$X_{s,i} = \sum_{j=1}^{i} \left(y_j - \langle y \rangle \right), \tag{3.4}$$

where $\langle y \rangle$ is the sample average of $\{y_i\}$. The range of the profile is given by

$$R_s = \max_{1 \leq i \leq s} X_{s,i} - \min_{1 \leq i \leq s} X_{s,i} \tag{3.5}$$

and the sample standard deviation is

$$S_s = \left[\frac{1}{n} \sum_{i=1}^{s} (y_j - \langle y \rangle)^2 \right]^{1/2}. \tag{3.6}$$

For a long-range correlated time series, it scales as a power law with respect to the time scale s

$$\lim_{s \to \infty} \frac{R(s)}{S(s)} \sim s^H, \tag{3.7}$$

where H is the Hurst exponent.

To distinguish between short memory and long memory, Lo (1991) proposed a modified R/S statistic, whose statistical behavior is invariant over a general class of short memory processes but deviates for long memory processes. Lo's (1991) modified R/S statistic reads

$$Q_s = R_s / \hat{S}_s(q), \tag{3.8}$$

where R_s is the range of profile defined in Eq. (3.5) and $\hat{S}_s(q)$ is defined by

$$\hat{S}_s^2(q) = S_s^2 + 2 \sum_{j=1}^{q} \omega_j(q) \rho_j = S_s^2 + 2 \sum_{j=1}^{q} \left(1 - \frac{j}{q-1} \right) \rho_j, \tag{3.9}$$

where S_s is the standard deviation defined in Eq. (3.6), $\omega_j(q) = 1 - \frac{j}{q+1}$ are weights, and

$$\rho_j = \frac{1}{n} \sum_{i=j+1}^{n} (y_i - \langle y \rangle)(y_{i-j} - \langle y \rangle) \tag{3.10}$$

is the autocovariance of the time series. If the time series is long-range correlated, the statistic variable

$$V_s(q) = \frac{1}{\sqrt{s}} Q_s(q) \tag{3.11}$$

has a finite positive value, whose cumulative distribution is

$$F(V) = 1 + 2 \sum_{k=1}^{\infty} (1 - 4k^2 V^2) e^{k^2 V^2}. \tag{3.12}$$

Lo (1991) proved that R_s trends to the Brownian bridge variable V_H, while the variable $S_s^2/(n\hat{S}_s(q))$ tends to 0 or ∞ for large q's, that is

$$V_s(q) = \frac{1}{\sqrt{s}} Q_n(q) = \begin{cases} 0, & H \in (0, 0.5) \\ \infty, & H \in (0.5, 1) \end{cases}. \tag{3.13}$$

Since the definition of the statistic $V_s(q)$ amounts to removing the autocorrelation up to q recurrence intervals, Teverovsky et al. (1999) found that the modified R/S test is biased since it tends to over-reject the presence of long memory.

3.2.2 Detrended Fluctuation Analysis

The detrended fluctuation analysis (DFA) was initially invented by Peng et al. (1994) to study the long-range dependent coding and noncoding DNA nucleotides sequence. In the original DFA method of Peng et al. (1994), the linear trend is removed. Kantelhardt et al. (2001) generalized the original DFA method by removing polynomial trends. It has soon been applied to various fields, including finance, and has become the most popular method for the detection of long-range correlations since it is easy to implement and provides robust estimation even for short time series (Audit et al., 2002; Montanari et al., 1999; Taqqu et al., 1995).

For a given recurrence interval time series $\{\tau_i | i = 1, \cdots, n\}$, we determine its profile $\{X_i | i = 1, \cdots, n\}$:

$$X_i = \sum_{j=1}^{i} \tau_j. \tag{3.14}$$

We then partition $\{X_i\}$ into $N_s = \lceil n/s \rceil$ nonoverlapping segments of size s, where $\lceil y \rceil$ is the smallest integer that is not smaller than y. The v-th segment is denoted as

$$S_v = \{X_{(v-1)s+j} | j = 1, \cdots, s\}. \tag{3.15}$$

For the s data points in each segment S_v, we estimate a polynomial of order ℓ by performing an OLS regression:

$$\widetilde{X}_{(v-1)s+j} = \sum_{k=0}^{\ell} a_k j^k, \tag{3.16}$$

which is the local trend of the profile. We then obtain the detrended residuals as follows:

$$\epsilon_{(v-1)s+j} = X_{(v-1)s+j} - \widetilde{X}_{(v-1)s+j} \tag{3.17}$$

for $j = 1, \cdots, s$.

The local detrended fluctuation function $F_v(s)$ associated with the v-th segment is defined as the r.m.s. of the detrended residuals:

$$F_v(s) = \left[\frac{1}{s} \sum_{i=1}^{s} \left[\epsilon_{(v-1)s+j} \right]^2 \right]^{\frac{1}{2}}. \tag{3.18}$$

The global detrended fluctuation function $F(s)$ is

$$F(s) = \left[\frac{1}{N_s} \sum_{v=1}^{N_s} F_v^2(s) \right]^{\frac{1}{2}} = \left(\frac{1}{n} \sum_{i=1}^{n} \epsilon_i^2 \right)^{\frac{1}{2}}, \tag{3.19}$$

which holds for $N_s = n/s$.

If $N_s > n/s$, the whole series $\{X_i\}$ cannot be completely covered by N_s boxes and the right-most segment is

$$S_{N_s} = \{X_{(N_s-1)s+j} | j = 1, 2, \cdots, n - N_s s\}. \tag{3.20}$$

In this case, one can use $2N_s = 2\mathrm{int}[N/s]$ boxes to cover the series from both ends of the time series and the two shorter segments at both ends of the residuals are discarded (Kantelhardt et al., 2002).

Varying the values of segment size s, we expect a power-law relation between the detrended fluctuation function $F(s)$ and the size scale s:

$$F(s) \sim s^H, \tag{3.21}$$

where H is the DFA exponent, an estimate of the Hurst exponent. If $H = 0.5$, the time series is uncorrelated. If $0.5 < H < 1.0$, the time series is long-term correlated or persistent. If $0 < H < 0.5$, the time series is anti-persistent. Taqqu et al. (1995) showed that, for fractional Gaussian noise and ARIMA process, Eq. (3.21) holds and H can be viewed as the Hurst exponent. The DFA exponent H is related to the power spectrum exponent η by $\eta = 2H - 1$ (Heneghan & McDarby, 2000; Talkner & Weber, 2000) and to the autocorrelation exponent μ by $\mu = 2 - 2H$ (Kantelhardt et al., 2001).

3.2.3 Detrending Moving Average Analysis

The detrending moving average (DMA) analysis was proposed by Alessio, Carbone, Castelli, and Frappietro (2002), which was motivated by the first-order moving average analysis that Vandewalle and Ausloos (1998) proposed for estimating the Hurst exponent of self-affinity signals. Essentially, DMA falls within the framework of DFA in the sense that DMA uses the moving average as the local trend (Carbone, 2009; Jiang et al., 2019). The DMA method has also been widely adopted to investigate the correlation structure of time series in diverse fields (Arianos & Carbone, 2007; Carbone & Castelli, 2003; Carbone et al., 2004a, 2004b; Matsushita et al., 2007; Serletis & Rosenberg, 2007, 2009; Varotsos et al., 2005). Cumulating evidence shows that the performance of DMA is comparable to DFA and sometimes better (Bashan et al., 2008; Jiang et al., 2019; Shao et al., 2012; Xu et al., 2005).

The main difference between the DFA and DMA methods lies in the determination of the local trend. In the DMA method, the moving average function $\widetilde{X}_i$ in a moving window of size s is adopted to detrend the profile (Arianos & Carbone, 2007), which reads

$$\widetilde{X}_i = \frac{1}{s} \sum_{k=-\lfloor (s-1)\theta \rfloor}^{\lceil (s-1)(1-\theta) \rceil} X_{i-k}, \tag{3.22}$$

where $\lfloor x \rfloor$ is the largest integer not greater than x, $\lceil x \rceil$ is the smallest integer not smaller than x, and $\theta \in [0,1]$ is the position parameter. Usually, we consider three representative versions of DMA: (1) The first case $\theta = 0$ refers to the backward moving average (BDMA) (Alessio et al., 2002; Xu et al., 2005); The second case $\theta = 0.5$ corresponds to the centered moving average (CDMA) (Xu et al., 2005), also termed MF-CMA (Schumann & Kantelhardt, 2011); and (3) The third case $\theta = 1$ is called the forward moving average (FDMA).

We stress that, in the determination of the moving averages, the window size must equal the segment size, as shown in Eq. (3.22); otherwise, the estimated DMA exponents is not correct (Gu & Zhou, 2010; Schumann & Kantelhardt, 2011).

3.2.4 Important Issues

When n/s is small, that is, when there are only a few segments, the estimation of the global fluctuation function is not reliable and may fluctuate remarkably. To solve this problem, we can adopt the resampling technique, which is based on random choices of segments of size s rather than covering the time series with adjacent boxes (Ji et al., 2009). This technique is also helpful for short time series.

Crossover phenomenon is ubiquitously observed in the scaling plots when we apply the DFA and DMA methods, which is usually due to some global trends in the profile of the time series (Jiang et al., 2019; Kantelhardt et al., 2001), such as polynomial trends, periodic trends, and power-law trends (Hu et al., 2001), or due to other factors such as nonlinearity (Chen, Ivanov, Hu, & Stanley, 2002). The crossover phenomenon may be explained by the superposition law in the fluctuation behavior for DFA Hu et al. (2001) and DMA Shao et al. (2015). When a crossover is observed in the scaling plots, one usually investigates the correlation behavior at short and long scales.

Mathematically, $H = 0.5$ corresponds to no correlations, while $H > 0.5$ indicates the presence of long memory. However, this is not true physically. It is vital to perform statistical tests to check if the estimated Hurst exponent is significantly different from 0.5 (Jiang et al., 2014). One can shuffle the time series to generate shuffled realizations and estimate their Hurst exponents. This bootstrapping technique allows us to estimate the p-value that quantifies if the estimated Hurst exponent of the raw time series differ from 0.5.

There are other important, but perhaps difficult, issues, such as the determination of the scaling range. We refer the readers to a review paper by Jiang et al. (2019).

3.3 Multifractal Nature

Multifractal nature corresponds to nonlinear long-range correlations (Bogachev et al., 2007). There are many methods for multifractal analysis (Jiang et al., 2019). Here, we describe two methods, multifractal detrended fluctuation analysis (MF-DFA) and multifractal detrending moving average analysis (MF-DMA), which are among the most utilized methods in econophysics.

The multifractal detrended fluctuation analysis is an extension of DFA, which was shortly developed independently by Castro e Silva and Moreira (1997), Weber and Talkner (2001), and Kantelhardt et al. (2002). Since the work of Kantelhardt et al. (2002), MF-DFA became very popular for multifractal analysis in various fields. On the other hand, Gu and Zhou (2010) generalized the DMA method for the investigation of the multifractal nature of time series and introduced the multifractal detrending moving average analysis.

In MF-DFA and MF-DMA, we calculate the qth-order overall detrended fluctuation as follows:

$$F_q(s) = \left\{ \frac{1}{N_s} \sum_{v=1}^{N_s} F_v^q(s) \right\}^{\frac{1}{q}}, \tag{3.23}$$

where q can take any real value except for $q = 0$. When $q = 0$, we have

$$\ln[F_0(s)] = \frac{1}{N_s} \sum_{v=1}^{N_s} \ln[F_v(s)], \tag{3.24}$$

according to L'Hôspital's rule.

Varying the values of segment size s, we can determine the power-law relation between the function $F_q(s)$ and the size scale s,

$$F_q(s) \sim s^{h(q)}. \tag{3.25}$$

According to the standard multifractal formalism, the multifractal scaling exponent $\tau(q)$ can be used to characterize the multifractal nature, which reads

$$\tau(q) = qh(q) - D_f, \tag{3.26}$$

where D_f is the fractal dimension of the geometric support of the multifractal measure (Kantelhardt et al., 2002). For time series analysis, we have $D_f = 1$. If the scaling exponent function $\tau(q)$ is a nonlinear function of q, the time series is regarded to have multifractal nature.

Oświęcimka et al. (2013) found that, in multifractal detrended fluctuation analysis, the obtained singularity spectrum might be very sensitive to the order of the detrending polynomial and the type of this sensitivity relation per se depends on the kind of analyzed time series. Certainty, the MFDMA method does not suffer this shortcoming.

There are also many subtle issues in the multifractal analysis of time series (Jiang et al., 2019). The most critical, but often ignored, problem is about the statistical tests for intrinsic multifractality. The results obtained from a multifractal analysis give the apparent multifractal nature, not the intrinsic multifractal behavior. Without nonlinear correlations, fat-tailedness and linear correlations only produce spurious multifractality (Bogachev et al., 2007; Drożdż et al., 2009; Zhou, 2009, 2012b). Recently, Gao et al. (2022) performed statistical tests on the presence of intrinsic multifractal nature through a systematic integration of various multifractality statistics.

4 Risk Estimation and Forecasting

4.1 Value at Risk

Value at Risk (VaR) is a statistic that quantifies the extent to which a company, portfolio, or position is likely to suffer financial losses over a specific time frame. This measure is most commonly used by investment and commercial banks to determine the extent and probability of potential losses in their institutional portfolios. Assuming that the distribution of the returns $\{r_i : i = 1, 2, \cdots, T\}$ of an asset is $p(r)$, VaR corresponds to the maximum possible losses for one given probability p^*,

$$p^* = \int_{-\infty}^{\mathrm{VaR}} p(r) dr. \tag{4.1}$$

There are three main ways of computing VaR: the historical method, the variance-covariance method, and the Monte Carlo simulation approach. Interestingly, the loss probability is the reciprocal of the mean recurrence interval, which provides an alternative expression for VaR (Ren & Zhou, 2010; Wang et al., 2007).

4.1.1 Loss Probability and Mean Recurrence Interval

Yamasaki et al. (2006) performed recurrence interval analysis on return losses. For a given threshold $Q < 0$, there are $N(r < Q)$ returns that are less than Q. Hence, the mean recurrence interval $\langle \tau \rangle$ is

$$\langle \tau \rangle = \frac{T}{N(r < Q)}. \tag{4.2}$$

By definition, we have

$$p^* = \frac{N(r < Q)}{T}. \tag{4.3}$$

Comparing Eq. (4.1) and Eq. (4.3), we have

$$Q = VaR. \tag{4.4}$$

Combining Eq. (4.2) and Eq. (4.3), we have

$$p^* = \frac{1}{\langle \tau \rangle}, \tag{4.5}$$

which shows that the inverse mean recurrence interval represents the loss probability p^*.

4.1.2 Returns with Power-law Tails

For high-frequency returns $r_{\Delta t}$ of stocks and indexes, the distribution can be well fitted by a Student's t distribution (Gu et al., 2008), whose tail is a power law (Gopikrishnan et al., 1998; Zhou, 2012a, 2012c):

$$p(r) = k|r|^{-(\delta+1)}, \tag{4.6}$$

where the exponent δ increases with Δt (Mu & Zhou, 2010). For Chinese stocks, Gu et al. (2008) found that the inverse cubic law holds. When Δt equals one minute, that is $\delta \approx 3$ (Gopikrishnan et al., 1998).

Substituting Eq. (4.6) into Eq. (4.1), we have

$$p^* = \frac{k}{\delta}|Q|^{-\delta}. \tag{4.7}$$

It follows that

$$\langle \tau \rangle = \frac{\delta}{k}|Q|^{\delta}, \tag{4.8}$$

which shows that there is a power-law dependence between the mean recurrence interval $\langle \tau \rangle$ and the threshold Q.

The above derivation remains true if we look at other financial variables that have a power-law distribution. These relationships have been empirically validated by F. Wang et al. (2007), Podobnik et al. (2009), and Ren and Zhou (2010) for a lot of assets.

4.1.3 Conditional Loss Probability $p^*_{|\tau_0}$

Wang et al. (2007) introduced the concept of conditional loss probability $p^*_{|\tau_0}$, which is the loss probability conditioned on the preceding recurrence interval τ_0. One can expect that:

$$p^*_{|\tau_0} = \frac{1}{\langle \tau | \tau_0 \rangle} = \int_{-\infty}^{Q} p(r|\tau_0)dr, \tag{4.9}$$

where $p^*_{|\tau_0}$ is the loss probability for a risk level of $VaR = Q < 0$ conditioned on the preceding interval τ_0 of losses below Q, $\langle \tau | \tau_0 \rangle$ is the mean conditional recurrence interval defined as the mean recurrence interval conditioned on the preceding interval τ_0, and $p(r|\tau_0)$ is the probability that a return r immediately follows interval τ_0.

Through recurrence interval analysis of the volatility time series of the 1-min prices of the 30 DJIA constituent stocks, the 10-min S&P 500 index prices, the daily prices of more than 6000 US stocks, the daily exchange rates of 35 other currencies to United States Dollar (USD), the daily spot prices of West Texas Intermediate (WTI) crude oil, and the daily gold prices (London P.M.), Wang et al. (2007) observed the following power-law relation:

$$\frac{\langle\tau|\tau_0\rangle}{\langle\tau\rangle} = A \left(\frac{\tau_0}{\langle\tau\rangle}\right)^\nu. \tag{4.10}$$

Together with Eq. (4.7), we have

$$\langle\tau|\tau_0\rangle = \frac{Ak^{\nu-1}}{\delta^{\nu-1}} \frac{\tau_0^\nu}{|Q|^{\delta(\nu-1)}}, \tag{4.11}$$

where A, δ, and k are fitted parameters. Inserting Eq. (4.10) into Eq. (4.9), we have

$$p^*_{|\tau_0} = \left(\frac{\tau_0}{\langle\tau\rangle}\right)^{-\nu} \frac{1}{A\langle\tau\rangle}. \tag{4.12}$$

Together with Eq. (4.7), we have

$$p^*_{|\tau_0} = \frac{\delta^{\nu-1}}{Ak^{\nu-1}} \frac{|Q|^{\delta(\nu-1)}}{\tau_0^\nu}. \tag{4.13}$$

If we know the preceding recurrence interval τ_0, we can estimate the risk level corresponding to a certain loss probability $p^*_{|\tau_0}$. Further, we find that

$$p^*_{|\tau_0} = \frac{(p^*)^{1-\nu}}{A\tau_0^\nu}. \tag{4.14}$$

Based on empirical analysis on the 1-min volatility time series of 20 liquid Chinese stocks, Ren and Zhou (2010) found that the scaled mean conditional recurrence interval $\langle\tau|\tau_0\rangle/\langle\tau\rangle$ can be fitted as a function of the scaled preceding interval $\tau_0/\langle\tau\rangle$ in the following form:

$$\frac{\langle\tau|\tau_0\rangle}{\langle\tau\rangle} = \left[1 + \mu \left(\frac{\tau_0}{\langle\tau\rangle}\right)^{-\gamma}\right]\left(\frac{\tau_0}{\langle\tau\rangle}\right)^\nu, \tag{4.15}$$

which holds in the medium region of $\tau_0/\langle\tau\rangle \in (0.1, 10]$. For large and small $\tau_0/\langle\tau\rangle$ values, $\langle\tau|\tau_0\rangle/\langle\tau\rangle$ diverges for different Q values and could not be fitted by Eq. (4.15). Comparing Eq. (4.15) and Eq. (4.10), we find that

$$A = 1 + \mu \left(\frac{\tau_0}{\langle\tau\rangle}\right)^{-\gamma}. \tag{4.16}$$

Substituting Eq. (4.15) into Eq. (4.9), we have

$$p^*_{|\tau_0} = \left[1 + \mu \left(\frac{\tau_0}{\langle \tau \rangle}\right)^{-\gamma}\right]^{-1} \left(\frac{\tau_0}{\langle \tau \rangle}\right)^{-\nu} \frac{1}{\langle \tau \rangle},$$ (4.17)

or, equivalently,

$$p^*_{|\tau_0} = \left[1 + \mu \left(\frac{k\tau_0}{\delta |Q|^\delta}\right)^{-\gamma}\right]^{-1} \left(\frac{k\tau_0}{\delta |Q|^\delta}\right)^{-\nu} \frac{k}{\delta |Q|^\delta}.$$ (4.18)

Similarly, the loss probability p^* and the conditional loss probability $p^*_{|\tau_0}$ are related as follows:

$$p^*_{|\tau_0} = \left[1 + \mu (\tau_0 p^*)^{-\gamma}\right]^{-1} (\tau_0 p^*)^{-\nu} p^*.$$ (4.19)

4.1.4 Generalization to Other Financial Variables

We note that VaR is defined for financial returns. However, the analysis framework is general and can be applied to other financial variables, such as volatility and trading volume.

Assume that we have a time series of financial volatility $\{v_i : i = 1, 2, \cdots, T\}$ whose distribution is $p(v)$. We are interested in the probability $p*$ that the volatility exceeds a given threshold Q. Mathematically, we have

$$p^* = \int_Q^\infty p(v) \mathrm{d}v.$$ (4.20)

The mean recurrence interval $\langle \tau \rangle$ is

$$\langle \tau \rangle = \frac{T}{N(v > Q)}.$$ (4.21)

By definition, we have

$$p^* = \frac{N(v > Q)}{T}.$$ (4.22)

Comparing Eq. (4.21) and Eq. (4.22), we have

$$p^* = \frac{1}{\langle \tau \rangle}.$$ (4.23)

Obviously, this relationship is "universal" for all time series. This expression implies that both p^* and $\langle \tau \rangle$ are measures of extreme fluctuation risks.

4.1.5 The Bogachev-Bunde Method

Bogachev and Bunde (2009a) proposed a new method (we call it the Bogachev-Bunde method) to improve the estimation of the VaR, which uses the local (instead of global) distribution of returns and integrates the hazard function $W(\Delta t | t)$.

4.2 Autoregressive Conditional Recurrence Interval Models

Recurrence interval analysis can be integrated into econometric regression models. Dai, Jiang, and Zhou (2018) considered the autoregressive conditional duration (ACD) model that is widely utilized to analyze irregular event durations. They further extended the model to a spatiotemporal autoregressive conditional duration (SACD) model by adding coupling spatial terms to the conditional duration structure. These considerations give a class of autoregressive conditional recurrence interval (ACRI) models.

4.2.1 The ACD Model

The ACD model was introduced by Engle and Russell (1998) to analyze dates that arrive at irregular intervals, which is an analog of the generalized autoregressive conditional heteroskedasticity (GARCH) model of Bollerslev (1986).

Let ψ_i be the expectation of the i duration τ_i, which is given by

$$E(\tau_i|\tau_{i-1}, \cdots, \tau_1; \theta) \equiv \psi_i \qquad (4.24)$$

and

$$\tau_i = \psi_i \epsilon_i, \qquad (4.25)$$

where $\{\epsilon_i\}$ is an independent and identically distributed random variable with density $p(\epsilon; \phi)$, and θ and ϕ are variation free.

The ACD(L_τ, L_ψ) model is specified as follows (Engle & Russell, 1998):

$$\psi_i = \omega + \sum_{j=1}^{L_\tau} \alpha_j \tau_{i-j} + \sum_{j=1}^{L_\psi} \beta_j \psi_{i-j}, \qquad (4.26)$$

where L_τ and L_ψ are the orders of the lags.

The ACD model can be extended to the logarithmic ACD model (Luc & Pierre, 2000; Lunde, 1999; Ng et al., 2014), or the Box-Cox transformation of Eq. (4.26) to make the model more adaptive (Hautsch, 2003). Different choices of the distribution $p(\epsilon)$ result in different ACD models (Engle & Russell, 1998). It can also be mapped onto the self-excited Hawkes process (Filimonov et al., 2015). Here we focus on the basic ACD model outlined above.

4.2.2 The Autoregressive Conditional Recurrence Interval Model

Dai et al. (2018) proposed the autoregressive conditional recurrence interval (ACRI) model, which is the RIA-based ACD model. For a given threshold Q, we define irregularly spaced extreme events whose magnitudes exceed Q. Hence, the recurrence intervals $\{\tau_{Q,i}|i = 1, \cdots, N_Q\}$ can be modelled by the ACD model. For each Q, we postulate that

$$\tau_{Q,i} = \psi_{Q,i}\epsilon_{Q,i}, \tag{4.27}$$

where $\{\epsilon_{Q,i}\}$ is an independent and identically distributed random variable, and $\psi_{Q,i}$ is the expectation of recurrence interval $\tau_{Q,i}$ when the information set $I_{Q,i-1}$ is known. Analogous to the ACD model, we specify that (Dai et al., 2018):

$$\psi_{Q,i} = \omega_Q \sum_{j=1}^{L_\tau} \alpha_{Q,j}\tau_{Q,i-j} + \sum_{j=1}^{L_\psi} \beta_{Q,j}\psi_{Q,i-j}. \tag{4.28}$$

The ACRI model can be extended to other ACD variants (Engle & Russell, 1998), such as the logarithmic ACD model (Luc & Pierre, 2000; Lunde, 1999; Ng et al., 2014) and the Box-Cox transformation of Eq. (4.28) (Hautsch, 2003).

4.2.3 The Multivariate Autoregressive Conditional Recurrence Interval Model

Consider a bunch of time series $\{x_i^{(u)}|i = 1, \cdots, T; u = 1, \cdots, U\}$, where u can be viewed as a node of a network. For a given threshold Q, we obtain the recurrence interval series $\{\tau_{Q,i}^{(u)}|i = 1, \cdots, N_Q; u = 1, \cdots, U\}$. Dai et al. (2018) proposed the multivariate autoregressive conditional recurrence interval (MACRI) model, which considers coupling terms in Eq. (4.28).

For two nodes u and v, Dai et al. (2018) defined node v's spatially reviewed recurrence intervals using node u's recurrence intervals as the time break point. As shown in Figure 4.1, for the recurrence interval $\tau_{Q,j}^{(u)}$ of u, v's spatially reviewed recurrence interval $\tau_{Q,j}^{(uv)}$ is the most recent recurrence interval of v that is no later than the ending time t of $\tau_{Q,j}^{(u)}$. In this definition, u is treated as a benchmark. When t is too small, such that an event occurred in u but not in v, we adopt the average recurrence interval of v as its spatially reviewed recurrence interval. In this way, we generate two recurrence interval series $\tau_{Q,j}^{(u)}$ and $\tau_{Q,j}^{(uv)}$ of the same length.

The multivariate autoregressive conditional recurrence interval (MACRI) model can be expressed as follows (Dai et al., 2018):

$$\tau_{Q,i}^{(u)} = \psi_{Q,i}^{(u)}\epsilon_{Q,i}^{(u)} \tag{4.29}$$

with

$$\psi_{Q,i}^{(u)} = \omega_Q^{(u)} + \sum_{j=1}^{L_\tau} \alpha_{Q,j}^{(u)}\tau_{Q,i-j}^{(u)} + \sum_{j=1}^{L_\psi} \beta_{Q,j}^{(u)}\psi_{Q,i-j}^{(u)}$$
$$+ \sum_{k=1}^{L_v} \sum_{v=1}^{N(u)} \mu_{q,v,k}^{(u)} w_{uv}\tau_{Q,i-k}^{(uv)}, \tag{4.30}$$

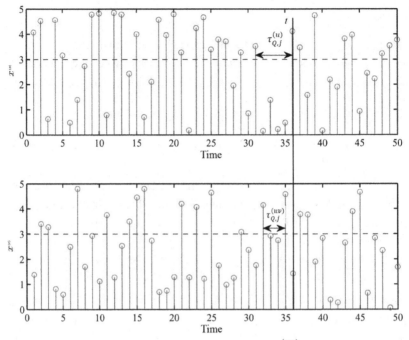

Figure 4.1 Spatially reviewed recurrence interval $\tau_{Q,j}^{(uv)}$ and its benchmark $\tau_{Q,j}^{(u)}$ for $Q = 3.0$.

where the coupling terms include the spatially reviewed recurrence intervals $\tau_{Q,i-k}^{(uv)}$ with k lags, and w_{uv} is the adjacent matrix or correlation matrix that is inversely related to the distance (Openshaw & Connolly, 1977). It is denoted as the MACRI(L_τ, L_ψ, L_v) model. Actually, w_{uv} can be viewed as a network, and thus the MACRI model can also be called a networked autoregressive conditional recurrence interval (NACRI) model.

4.2.4 The MACRI (1, 1, 1) Model

We consider the simplest MACRI(1, 1, 1) model, which takes into consideration the nearest neighbor $NN(i)$ of location i, with one lag behind. In this case, $w_{ij} = 1$ when $|i - j| = 1$ and zero otherwise. Hence, Eq. (4.30) reduces to

$$\psi_{Q,i}^{(u)} = \omega_Q^{(u)} + \alpha_{Q,1}^{(u)}\tau_{Q,i-1}^{(u)} + \beta_{Q,1}^{(u)}\psi_{Q,i-1}^{(u)} + \mu_{q,1,1}^{(u)}\tau_{Q,i-1}^{(NN(i))} \tag{4.31}$$

This simplified multivariate autoregressive conditional duration model can also be denoted as the RIA-M-ACD(1,1,1) model, and the model without the coupling terms is hence categorized as the RIA-ACD(1,1) model.

It follows from Eq. (4.31) that

$$
\begin{cases}
\psi_{Q,i}^{(u)} = \omega_Q^{(u)} + \alpha_{Q,1}^{(u)}\tau_{Q,i-1}^{(u)} + \beta_{Q,1}^{(u)}\psi_{Q,i-1}^{(u)} + \mu_{q,1,1}^{(u)}\tau_{Q,i-1}^{(uv)} \\
\psi_{Q,i}^{(v)} = \omega_Q^{(v)} + \alpha_{Q,1}^{(v)}\tau_{Q,i-1}^{(v)} + \beta_{Q,1}^{(v)}\psi_{Q,i-1}^{(v)} + \mu_{q,1,1}^{(v)}\tau_{Q,i-1}^{(vu)}
\end{cases}.
\tag{4.32}
$$

where $E\left[\tau_{Q,i}^{(u)}\right] = \psi_{Q,i}^{(u)}$ and $E\left[\tau_{Q,i}^{(v)}\right] = \psi_{Q,i}^{(v)}$. The expectation of the recurrence interval of node u is

$$
E\left[\tau_Q^{(u)}\big|(v)\right] = \frac{\omega_Q^{(v)}\mu_{Q,1,1}^{(u)} + \omega_Q^{(u)}\left(1 - \alpha_{Q,1}^{(v)} - \beta_{Q,1}^{(v)}\right)}{\left(1 - \alpha_{Q,1}^{(u)} - \beta_{Q,1}^{(u)}\right)\left(1 - \alpha_{Q,1}^{(v)} - \beta_{Q,1}^{(v)}\right) - \mu_{Q,1,1}^{(u)}\mu_{Q,1,1}^{(v)}}.
\tag{4.33}
$$

If node v's recurrence intervals between extreme events have no impact on u's conditional intervals, we have $\mu_{q,1,1}^{(u)} = 0$. It follows that

$$
E\left[\tau_Q^{(u)}\big|(j)\right] = \frac{\omega_q^{(u)}}{1 - \alpha_{Q,1}^{(u)} - \beta_{Q,1}^{(u)}} \triangleq \gamma_u.
\tag{4.34}
$$

Under weak stationary conditions, the expected intervals will reduce to classic ACD expectations. If node u doesn't influence v, but the other way around, we have $\mu_{Q,1,1}^{(v)} = 0$. It follows that

$$
\begin{aligned}
E\left[\tau_Q^{(u)}\big|(v)\right] &= \frac{\omega_Q^{(u)}}{1 - \alpha_{Q,1}^{(u)} - \beta_{Q,1}^{(u)}} + \frac{\omega_q^{(v)}}{1 - \alpha_{Q,1}^{(v)} - \beta_{Q,1}^{(v)}} \frac{\mu_{Q,1,1}^{(u)}}{1 - \alpha_{Q,1}^{(u)} - \beta_{Q,1}^{(u)}} \\
&= \gamma_u + \gamma_v \frac{\mu_{Q,1,1}^{(u)}}{1 - \alpha_{Q,1}^{(u)} - \beta_{Q,1}^{(u)}}.
\end{aligned}
\tag{4.35}
$$

Hence, the first term is a noncoupling term, and the second is the coupling interaction triggered intervals.

The next model specification is the distribution of the innovation sequence $\{\epsilon_{Q,i}\}$. With a decreasing trend in the recurrence intervals' histogram, we resort to the exponential distribution

$$
f(\epsilon) = e^{-\epsilon}
\tag{4.36}
$$

and the Weibull distribution

$$
f(\epsilon) = \frac{c}{\lambda}\left(\frac{\epsilon}{\lambda}\right)^{c-1} e^{-(\epsilon/\lambda)^c}.
\tag{4.37}
$$

In other words, small intervals are more likely than large intervals whatever the threshold Q is. It should be pointed out that in order to make the Weibull distribution take on this trend, we restrict Weibull's shape parameter c in $(0, 1)$. Since $E\left[\epsilon_{Q,i}^{(u)}\right] = 1$, we obtain that

$$\lambda = \frac{1}{\Gamma(1 + 1/k)}. \tag{4.38}$$

Therefore, the Weibull distribution becomes

$$f(\epsilon) = k\Gamma(1 + 1/k)[\epsilon\Gamma(1 + 1/k)]^{k-1}\exp\left[-(\epsilon\Gamma(1 + 1/k))^k\right]. \tag{4.39}$$

Denoting $D_Q^{(u)} = \left\{d_{Q,1}^{(u)}, d_{Q,2}^{(u)}, \cdots, d_{Q,N}^{(u)}\right\}$ as the realizations of the MACRI $(1,1,1)$ model and $\theta_Q^{(u)} = \left(\omega_Q^{(u)}, \alpha_{Q,1}^{(u)}, \beta_{Q,1}^{(u)}, \mu_{Q,1,1}^{(u)}\right)$ as the parameter set, the likelihood function of the recurrence interval realizations is

$$p\left(D_Q^{(u)}\middle|\theta_Q^{(u)}\right) = p\left(\tau_{Q,1}^{(u)}\middle|\theta_Q^{(u)}\right)\prod_{i=2}^{N}p\left(\tau_{Q,i}^{(u)}\middle|\tau_{Q,i-1}^{(u)}, \theta_Q^{(u)}\right). \tag{4.40}$$

The conditional log likelihood function of the data becomes

$$L\left(\theta_Q^{(u)}\middle|D_Q^{(u)}\right) = -\sum_{i=2}^{N}\log\left[p\left(\tau_{Q,i}^{(u)}\middle|\tau_{Q,i-1}^{(u)}, \theta_Q^{(u)}\right)\right]. \tag{4.41}$$

For the exponential distribution, we have

$$p\left(\tau_{Q,i}^{(u)}\middle|\tau_{Q,i-1}^{(u)}, \theta_Q^{(u)}\right) = \frac{1}{\psi_{Q,i}^{(u)}}\exp\left[-\frac{\tau_{Q,i}^{(u)}}{\psi_{Q,i}^{(u)}}\right]. \tag{4.42}$$

For the Weibull distribution, similarly, we have

$$p\left(\tau_{Q,i}^{(u)}\middle|\tau_{Q,i-1}^{(u)}, \theta_Q^{(u)}\right) = \frac{c}{\psi_{Q,i}^{(u)}}\Gamma\left(1 + \frac{1}{c}\right)\left[\frac{\tau_{Q,i}^{(u)}}{\psi_{Q,i}^{(u)}}\Gamma\left(1 + \frac{1}{c}\right)\right]^{c-1}$$

$$\times \exp\left[-\left(\frac{\tau_{Q,i}^{(u)}}{\psi_{Q,i}^{(u)}}\Gamma\left(1 + \frac{1}{c}\right)\right)^c\right]. \tag{4.43}$$

The estimate of $\hat{\theta}_Q^{(u)}$ can be obtained by maximizing $L\left(\theta_Q^{(u)}\middle|D_Q^{(u)}\right)$ analytically or numerically.

The standard errors of the estimates are obtained through the Fisher information matrix. In view of the effect of serial correlation and heteroskedasticity, we adopt the Newey-West robust standard errors by correcting the residuals with the weight of $1 - i/N$ (Newey & West, 1987).

Similar to the classic ACD model, we use the Ljung-Box Q as a test statistic from the model of Ljung and Box (1978):

$$Q_Q^{(u)}(L) = N(N+2) \sum_{k=1}^{L} \frac{\rho_{\epsilon_Q^{(u)}}^2(k)}{N-k}, \tag{4.44}$$

where $\rho_{\epsilon_Q^{(u)}}(k)$ is the k-th lag autocorrelation of $\epsilon_Q^{(u)}$. If the fitted model is adequate, the standardized innovation $\epsilon_Q^{(u)}$ should take on an i.i.d. sequence of random variables with the assumed distribution. Therefore, there will be no serial correlations detected from the innovations and $Q_Q^{(u)}(L)$ is insignificant. Although some drawbacks have been pinpointed and other statistics are proposed (Bagnato et al., 2017), the Q-test is still the most popular one to check the autocorrelations of the residuals.

4.3 Hazard Probability

On the other hand, the empirical hazard function W_{emp} can be evaluated as follows:

$$W_{\text{emp}}(\Delta t | t) = \frac{\#(t < \tau \leq t + \Delta t)}{\#(\tau > t)}, \tag{4.45}$$

where the denominator $\#(\tau > t)$ is the number of recurrence intervals whose values are greater than t, and the numerator $\#(t < \tau \leq t + \Delta t)$ is the number of recurrence intervals which locate in the range of $(t, t + \Delta t]$.

We use the hazard probability $W(\Delta t | t)$ to forecast the occurrence of large volatility events. The $W(\Delta t | t)$ is the probability that there will be additional waiting time Δt before another large volatility event occurs when the previous large volatility event occurred t time ago, which can be formulated as (Bogachev et al., 2007; Sornette & Knopoff, 1997),

$$W(\Delta t | t) = \frac{\int_t^{t+\Delta t} p(t)dt}{\int_t^{\infty} p(t)dt}, \tag{4.46}$$

where $p(t)$ is the probability distribution of the recurrence intervals between extreme events. By definition, the cumulative distribution function $C(t)$ of $p(t)$ is

$$C(t) = \int_0^t p(t)dt. \tag{4.47}$$

Eq. (4.46) can also be expressed as follows (Bogachev & Bunde, 2009b):

$$W(\Delta t | t) = \frac{C(t + \Delta t) - C(t)}{1 - C(t)}. \tag{4.48}$$

This probability is the key early-warning measurement for the occurrence of extreme events. The early warning is triggered when the probability $W(\Delta t|t)$ is greater than a predefined hazard threshold. We can theoretically derive this hazard probability if we have the distribution of the recurrence intervals between consecutive extreme events.

If we designate the top 1% of volatility values (corresponding to the mean recurrence time $\langle \tau \rangle = 100$) to be extreme events, we can estimate the hazard probability $W_q(\Delta t, t)$ in t when fixing Δt. The recurrence intervals between events with $\langle \tau \rangle = 100$ are well approximated by the stretched exponential distribution for most stocks. This allows us to approach the theoretical hazard probability $W_q(\Delta t, t)$ in terms of the stretched exponential distribution. By substituting equation (2.15) into Eq. (4.46), we obtain

$$W_{\mathrm{SE}}(\Delta t|t) = \frac{\frac{b\gamma}{a} - \Gamma_l\left(\frac{1}{\gamma}, (bt)^\gamma\right) - \Gamma_u\left(\frac{1}{\gamma}, [b(t + \Delta t)]^\gamma\right)}{\Gamma_u\left(\frac{1}{\gamma}, (bt)^\gamma\right)}, \qquad (4.49)$$

where $\Gamma_l(s, x)$ and $\Gamma_u(s, x)$ are lower and upper incomplete gamma function, respectively, and a and b are in dependent of γ.

4.3.1 Exponential Distribution

For uncorrelated time series, the recurrence intervals are distributed exponentially, and the cumulative distribution function is

$$C_{\mathrm{Exp}}(\Delta t|t) = 1 - \exp\left[-\frac{t}{\langle \tau \rangle}\right], \qquad (4.50)$$

Substituting Eq. (2.4) into Eq. (4.46) or substituting Eq. (4.50) into Eq. (4.48), we have

$$W_{\mathrm{Exp}}(\Delta t|t) = 1 - \exp\left[-\frac{\Delta t}{\langle \tau \rangle}\right], \qquad (4.51)$$

which is independent of t. When $\Delta t/\langle \tau \rangle \ll 1$, we can take the first-order approximation of the Taylor expansion and obtain that

$$W_{\mathrm{Exp}}(\Delta t|t) = \frac{\Delta t}{\langle \tau \rangle}, \qquad (4.52)$$

which implies that, for a given threshold Q, the hazard probability $W_{\mathrm{exp}}(\Delta t|t)$ is proportional to Δt.

4.3.2 Power-law Distribution

The cumulative distribution function of the power-law distribution given in Eq. (2.5) is

$$C(t) = \left(\frac{t}{\langle\tau\rangle}\right)^{1-\alpha} \tag{4.53}$$

such that the hazard function is (Bogachev et al., 2007)

$$W_{\text{PL}}(\Delta t|t) \approx 1 - \left(1 + \frac{\Delta t}{t}\right)^{1-\alpha}. \tag{4.54}$$

When $\Delta t \ll t$, we have

$$W_{\text{PL}}(\Delta t|t) \approx (\alpha - 1)\frac{\Delta t}{t}. \tag{4.55}$$

The probability $W_{\text{PL}}(\Delta t|t)$ is found to be proportional to Δt and inversely proportional to t. When there is scaling behavior, that is, α is independent of Q, $W_{\text{PL}}(\Delta t|t)$ is independent of the threshold Q or the mean recurrence interval $\langle\tau\rangle$.

4.3.3 Power-law Distribution with an Exponential Cutoff

The power-law distribution with an exponential cutoff is given in Eq. (2.7):

$$p_{\text{PLExp}}(\tau) = c\tau^{-\beta-1}e^{-k\tau}, \tag{4.56}$$

where k and c are expressed in Eq. (2.8) and Eq. (2.9), respectively. Its cumulative distribution function is written as,

$$C_{\text{PLExp}}(t) = \int_0^t c\tau^{-\beta-1}e^{-k\tau}\mathrm{d}\tau = ck^\beta \int_0^{kt} s^{-\beta-1}e^{-s}\mathrm{d}s = ck^\beta\Gamma_l(-\beta, kt), \tag{4.57}$$

where $s = k\tau$, and Γ_l has the form of (but is not) the lower incomplete gamma function.

By putting the cumulative probability distribution function Eqs. (4.57) into Eq. (4.46), we obtain the hazard probability $W_{\text{PLExp}}(\Delta t|t)$ for power-law distribution with an exponential function

$$W_{\text{PLExp}}(\Delta t|t) = \frac{\Gamma_l(-\beta, k(t+\Delta t)) - \Gamma_l(-\beta, kt)}{k^{-\beta}/c - \Gamma_l(-\beta, kt)}. \tag{4.58}$$

4.3.4 Double Power-law Distribution

When $t > r_c$, simple algebraic manipulation leads to

$$W_{\text{DPL}}(\Delta t|t) \simeq (\alpha_2 - 1)\Delta t/t, \tag{4.59}$$

which is the same as Eq. (4.55). For the recurrence intervals of energy dissipation rate in three-dimensional fully developed turbulence, an intriguing feature is that $W_{\text{DPL}}(\Delta t|t)$ is independent of the threshold Q, which is a direct consequence of the scaling behavior of $P_Q(r)$ (Liu et al., 2009).

When $t < r_c$, we obtain that

$$W_{\text{DPL}}(\Delta t|t) \approx \frac{(\alpha_1 - 1)\left(\frac{t}{\langle\tau\rangle}\right)^{-\alpha_1}\frac{\Delta t}{\langle\tau\rangle}}{\left(\frac{t}{\langle\tau\rangle}\right)^{1-\alpha_1} - \left(\frac{t_c}{\langle\tau\rangle}\right)^{1-\alpha_1} + \frac{A_2}{A_1}\frac{\alpha_1-1}{\alpha_2-1}\left(\frac{t_c}{\langle\tau\rangle}\right)^{1-\alpha_2}}. \tag{4.60}$$

We find that $W_{\text{DPL}}(\Delta t|t)$ is proportional to Δt. However, $W_{\text{DPL}}(\Delta t|t)$ also depends on $\langle\tau\rangle$. Since $W_{\text{DPL}}(\Delta t|t)$ should be continuous at $t = r_c$, combining Eqs. (4.59) and (4.60), we have

$$(\alpha_2 - 1)\frac{\Delta t}{t_c} = \frac{(\alpha_1 - 1)\left(\frac{t_c}{\langle\tau\rangle}\right)^{-\alpha_1}\frac{\Delta t}{\langle\tau\rangle}}{\left(\frac{t_c}{\langle\tau\rangle}\right)^{1-\alpha_1} - \left(\frac{t_c}{\langle\tau\rangle}\right)^{1-\alpha_1} + \frac{A_2}{A_1}\frac{\alpha_1-1}{\alpha_2-1}\left(\frac{t_c}{\langle\tau\rangle}\right)^{1-\alpha_2}}. \tag{4.61}$$

$$= \frac{(\alpha_1 - 1)\left(\frac{t_c}{\langle\tau\rangle}\right)^{-\alpha_1}\frac{\Delta t}{\langle\tau\rangle}}{\frac{A_2}{A_1}\frac{\alpha_1-1}{\alpha_2-1}\left(\frac{t_c}{\langle\tau\rangle}\right)^{1-\alpha_2}}. \tag{4.62}$$

It follows that

$$t_c/\langle\tau\rangle = (A_2/A_1)^{1/(\alpha_2-\alpha_1)}. \tag{4.63}$$

Since $A_1 < A_2$ and $\alpha_1 < \alpha_2$, we have

$$t_c > \langle\tau\rangle. \tag{4.64}$$

4.3.5 Stretched Exponential Distribution

The stretched exponential distribution is given in Eq. (2.15):

$$p_{\text{SE}}(\tau) = ae^{-(b\tau)^\gamma}, \tag{4.65}$$

where $a = \frac{\gamma\Gamma(2/\gamma)}{\Gamma(1/\gamma)^2\tau_Q}$ and $b = \frac{\Gamma(2/\gamma)}{\Gamma(1/\gamma)\tau_Q}$. Its cumulative distribution function is written as,

$$C_{\text{SE}}(t) = \int_0^t ae^{-(b\tau)^\gamma}\,d\tau = \frac{\int_0^{(bt)^\gamma} s^{\frac{1}{\gamma}-1}e^{-s}ds}{\Gamma\left(\frac{1}{\gamma}\right)} = \frac{\Gamma_l\left(\frac{1}{\gamma},(bt)^\gamma\right)}{\Gamma\left(\frac{1}{\gamma}\right)}, \tag{4.66}$$

where $s = (b\tau)^\gamma$ and Γ_l is the lower incomplete gamma function. By putting the cumulative probability distribution function Eq. (4.66) into Eq. (4.46), we obtain the hazard probability W_{SE} for the stretched exponential distribution,

$$W_{\text{SE}}(\Delta t|t) = \frac{\Gamma_l\left(\frac{1}{\gamma},[b(t+\Delta t)]^\gamma\right) - \Gamma_l\left(\frac{1}{\gamma},(bt)^\gamma\right)}{\mu\left(\frac{1}{\gamma}\right) - \Gamma_l\left(\frac{1}{\gamma},(bt)^\gamma\right)}. \tag{4.67}$$

4.3.6 q-exponential Distribution

The q-exponential distribution is given in Eq. (2.11):

$$P_{qExp}(\tau) = (2 - q)\lambda[1 + (q - 1)\lambda\tau]^{-\frac{1}{q-1}}, \qquad (4.68)$$

where $\lambda = \frac{1}{\tau_Q(3-2q)}$. And its cumulative distribution function is written as,

$$C_{qExp}(t) = \int_0^t (2-q)\lambda[1+(q-1)\lambda\tau]^{-\frac{1}{q-1}} d\tau = 1-[1+(q-1)\lambda t]^{1-\frac{1}{q-1}}, \qquad (4.69)$$

By putting the cumulative probability distribution function Eqs. (4.69) into Eq. (4.46), we obtain the hazard probability $W_{qE}(\Delta t|t)$ for q-exponential distribution (Ludescher, Tsallis, & Bunde, 2011),

$$W_{qExp}(\Delta t|t) = 1 - \left[1 + \frac{(q - 1)\lambda\Delta t}{1 + (q - 1)\lambda t}\right]^{1-\frac{1}{q-1}}. \qquad (4.70)$$

4.3.7 Weibull Distribution

The Weibull distribution is given in Eq. (2.13):

$$P_{WBL}(\tau) = \frac{\zeta}{d}\left(\frac{\tau}{d}\right)^{\zeta-1} \exp\left[-\left(\frac{\tau}{d}\right)^{\zeta}\right]. \qquad (4.71)$$

where $d = \frac{\langle\tau\rangle}{\Gamma(1+1/\zeta)}$. Its cumulative distribution function is a stretched exponential distribution (Laherrère & Sornette, 1998):

$$C(\tau) = 1 - \exp\left[-\left(\frac{\tau}{d}\right)^{\zeta}\right], \qquad (4.72)$$

Substituting Eq. (4.72) into Eq. (4.48), we obtain the hazard probability $W_W(\Delta t|t)$ for the Weibull distribution (Jiang et al., 2018; Yakovlev et al., 2006),

$$W_{WBL}(\Delta t|t) = \frac{\exp\left[-\left(\frac{t}{d}\right)^{\zeta}\right] - \exp\left[-\left(\frac{t+\Delta t}{d}\right)^{\zeta}\right]}{\exp\left[-\left(\frac{t}{d}\right)^{\zeta}\right]} = 1 - \frac{\exp\left[-\left(\frac{t+\Delta t}{d}\right)^{\zeta}\right]}{\exp\left[-\left(\frac{t}{d}\right)^{\zeta}\right]}. \qquad (4.73)$$

4.3.8 Stretched Weibull Distribution

The cumulative distribution function of the stretched Weibull distribution in Eq. (2.20) is (Bogachev & Bunde, 2009b)

$$C(t) = 1 - \exp\left[-\lambda\left(\frac{t}{\langle\tau\rangle}\right)^{\mu-1}\right]. \qquad (4.74)$$

The hazard function is

$$
W_{\text{strWBL}}(\Delta t|t) = \frac{\exp\left[-\lambda\left(\frac{t}{\langle\tau\rangle}\right)^{\mu-1}\right] - \exp\left[-\lambda\left(\frac{t+\Delta t}{\langle\tau\rangle}\right)^{\mu-1}\right]}{1 - \exp\left[-\lambda\left(\frac{t}{\langle\tau\rangle}\right)^{\mu-1}\right]}.
\tag{4.75}
$$

When $\Delta t \ll t$, we have

$$
W_{\text{strWBL}}(\Delta t|t) = C_1 \frac{\Delta t}{\langle\tau\rangle}\left(\frac{t}{\langle\tau\rangle}\right)^{\mu-1},
\tag{4.76}
$$

where $C_1 = \mu\lambda$ is the normalization constant (Bogachev & Bunde, 2009b).

4.3.9 Power-law Distribution with an Exponential Cutoff

For fixed Δt, all three hazard probabilities decrease as t increases, which explains the clustering of extremes in financial returns and volatilities. Bogachev and Bunde (2009b, 2011) and Bunde et al. (2012) also derive an approximation of the hazard function when the recurrence intervals are distributed as a power law with an exponential tail. Especially in Bunde et al. (2012), two additional distributions including the power law with stretched exponentially tailed distribution and purely power law distribution are further utilized to give the approximate forms of hazard function.

4.4 Quantification of Predictive Performance

4.4.1 Receiver Operating Characteristics

Having the hazard probability $W(\Delta t|t)$ in hand, in order to label the signals, we need to choose a threshold w_t such that

$$
E(t) = \begin{cases} 1 & \text{if } W(\Delta t|t) > w_t \\ 0 & \text{otherwise} \end{cases},
\tag{4.77}
$$

where $E(t) = 1$ means that an extreme event is forecast to occur.

We need to quantify the performance of the predictor. Following the receiver operating characteristics (ROC) analysis (Fawcett, 2006), after comparing the forecasted extremes with the actual events, each time point can be classified into four categories:

(1) True positive: a correct prediction of an extreme event,
(2) True negative: a correct prediction of no extreme event,
(3) False negative: a missed event that occurs but is not predicted,
(4) False positive: a false alarm predicting the occurrence of an extreme event that does not occur.

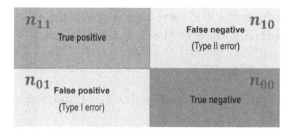

Figure 4.2 Confusion matrix.

These outcomes form the confusion matrix as illustrated in Figure 4.2. Among them, false positive is the Type I error, while false negative is the Type II error.

We count the numbers in each category and denote that n_{11} is the number of extreme events that are correctly predicted, n_{00} is the number of nonextreme events that are correctly predicted, n_{01} is the number of missed events, and n_{10} is the number of false alarms. The true positive rate (also called hit rate and recall) D is calculated as follows:

$$D = \frac{n_{11}}{n_{10} + n_{11}}, \tag{4.78}$$

while the false-positive rate (also called false alarm rate) A is determined as follows:

$$A = \frac{n_{01}}{n_{00} + n_{01}}. \tag{4.79}$$

Varying the w_t range from 0 to 1, we obtain different pairs of (D, A). Plotting D with respect to A, we obtain the ROC. If $w_t = 0$, all the time points are predicted to have extreme events, which means that $n_{10} = n_{00} = 0$. It follows that $D = A = 1$. If $w_t = 1$, all the time points are predicted to have no extreme events, which means that $n_{11} = n_{01} = 0$. It follows that $D = A = 0$. Therefore, the ROC curve connects the point $(0, 0)$ at the left bottom corner to the point $(1, 1)$ at the right top corner. When the predictor is a random guess, we have $D = A$, resulting in a straight line between the two corners.

4.4.2 Area Under the ROC Curve

The overall predictive performance can be quantified by the area under the ROC curve (AUC) (Fawcett, 2006). In practice, people often favor predicting models with fewer false alarms. Hence, Jiang et al. (2016) suggested to define the following performance statistics to evaluate the predicting power,

$$\text{AUC}_m = \int_0^{0.3} D(A) dA, \tag{4.80}$$

which is the area under the ROC curve in the range of $0 \leq A \leq 0.3$. If the model is a random predictor, we have $D(A) = A$, such that

$$\text{AUC}_m = \int_0^{0.3} A \, dA = 0.045. \tag{4.81}$$

If the model is a perfect predictor, we have $D(A) = 1$, such that

$$\text{AUC}_m = \int_0^{0.3} dA = 0.3. \tag{4.82}$$

Therefore, the statistic AUC_m locates in the range of $[0.045, 0.3]$.

4.4.3 Usefulness of Extreme Forecasts

In order to find a balanced signal between Type I and Type II errors, following Alessi and Detken (2011), we can define a loss function:

$$L(\theta) = \theta(1 - D) + (1 - \theta)A. \tag{4.83}$$

The parameter θ is the investor preference for avoiding either Type I or Type II errors (El-Shagi, Knedlik, & von Schweinitz, 2013). We can further define the usefulness of extreme forecasts as follows:

$$U(\theta) = \min(\theta, 1 - \theta) - L(\theta), \tag{4.84}$$

where $\min(\theta, 1-\theta)$ is the loss faced by investors when they ignore the predictive signals, and $U(\theta)$ is the extent to which the extreme forecasting model offers better performance than no model at all (Betz et al., 2014). Extreme forecasts are deemed useful if $U(\theta) > 0$, which means that the losses using the forecasts are lower than when the forecasts are ignored. The usefulness of extreme forecasts ignores any influence from the data imbalance, that is, that nonextreme events occur much more frequently than extreme events (Betz et al., 2014; Sarlin, 2013).

Given the hazard probability $W(\Delta t | t)$, we need a hazard threshold w_t that maximizes the usefulness $U(\theta)$ (Babecký et al., 2014; Betz et al., 2014; Duca & Peltonen, 2013). Christensen and Li (2014) optimized the threshold by minimizing the noise-to-signal ratio D/A. When we optimize the usefulness function, there is a marginal rate of substitution between Type I and Type II errors, but this marginal rate is not clear in the optimization of the noise-to-signal ratio, and this can result in an unacceptable level of Type I and Type II errors (Alessi & Detken, 2011; Babecký et al., 2014; El-Shagi et al., 2013).

4.4.4 KSS Test

Alternatively, we can follow Gresnigt, Kole, and Franses (2015) and use the Hanssen-Kuiper skill score (KSS) to assess the validity of extreme forecasts.

The KSS is the difference $D - A$ between the correct prediction rate and the false alarm rate. The KSS encompasses both missing occurrence errors and false alarm errors. Decreasing these two errors increases the value of KSS.

5 Empirical Results and Theoretical Analyses

5.1 Financial Volatility

Consider a price time series $\{P(t) : t = 1, \cdots, T\}$ of a financial asset. The logarithmic return over timescale Δt is defined as follows:

$$r(t; \Delta t) = \ln P(t) - \ln P(t - \Delta t). \tag{5.1}$$

Although there are variant definitions for volatility in finance (Bollen & Inder, 2002; Garman & Klass, 1980), econophysicists usually adopt the simplest definition

$$v(t; \Delta t) = |r(t; \Delta t)|, \tag{5.2}$$

which is the absolute return. Without being specifically noted, "volatility" refers to this definition throughout this Element. We will also drop Δt if only one timescale is considered in the studies.

For high-frequency intraday volatility, there is an intraday pattern:

$$A(s) = \frac{1}{D} \sum_{d=1}^{D} v_d(s), \tag{5.3}$$

which is the average volatility at a specific moment s of the day over all D trading days, and $v_d(s)$ is the s-th volatility in day d. The U-shaped pattern in intraday volatility has been well documented by Wood, McInish, and Ord (1985) and Harris (1986), showing that volatility is high at the open and close of trading and low in the middle of the day. One can remove the intraday pattern before further analysis:

$$v(t) / A(s) \rightarrow v(t). \tag{5.4}$$

If we do not remove the intraday pattern, there will be a crossover phenomenon in the recurrence interval distributions. In most studies, the volatility time series is further normalized by its standard deviation or root-mean-square.

5.1.1 Power-law Distributions

Kaizoji and Kaizoji (2004) investigated the recurrence interval (they termed calm-time interval) distributions of the daily volatility time series for the Nikkei 225 index and 800 companies listed on the Tokyo Stock Exchange from January 4, 1975, to December 28, 2001. They found that the recurrence intervals for individual time series are distributed according to power laws $p(\tau) \sim \tau^{-1-\delta}$, whose exponent δ monotonically decreases with respect to the threshold Q. Fixing the threshold Q, the power-law exponents δ differ for different time series. Kitt and Kalda (2005) reported similar results for a few currencies and stock market indices.

Yamasaki et al. (2005) investigated the recurrence intervals of daily volatility records of seven stocks and seven currencies and found the appearance of power-law distributions. They further found that $\delta = 1$ for all time series and for different thresholds, which suggest the scaled probability function $\langle\tau\rangle p_Q(\tau)$ can be well approximated by the same universal power law with the exponent $\delta = 1$. Ouyang et al. (2014) investigated the daily volatility time series of 259 stocks for the stock markets in Shanghai (SH), Shenzhen (SZ), Taiwan (TW) and Hong Kong (HK). For a given threshold Q and for each market, they obtained the recurrence intervals of each stock and put all intervals of the 259 stocks together. They reported a power-law scaling in the distributions with $\alpha = 3.0$ for SH, 3.1 for SZ, 3.2 for TW, and 3.2 for HK.

Lee et al. (2006) performed recurrence interval analysis of the 1-min volatility time series of the Korean stock market index KOSPI from 30 March 1992 to 30 November 1999. They observed a crossover phenomenon with the crossover time being 200 minutes. This is actually caused by the U-shaped pattern in intraday volatility as documented by Wood et al. (1985) and Harris (1986), showing that volatility is high at the open and close of trading and low in the middle of the day. Hence, the crossover time is more likely to be one trading day. Lee et al. (2006) also reported the presence of power-law tails for the recurrence intervals greater than the crossover time, whose tail exponent δ does not depend on the threshold Q but decreases when the timescale Δt used to define volatility increases indicating longer tails for large Δt. These findings have been confirmed by Hong et al. (2007) for $\Delta t = 1$ min, 10 min, 30 min, 60 min, and 600 min.

Li and Liaw (2015) analyzed the 1-min volatility time series of 10 stock indexes (Australia AORD, Brazil BVSP, China SSEC, France CAC40, Germany DAX, India SENSEX, Japan NIKKEI 225, Portugal PSI20, Taiwan TAIEX, and the USA S&P 500) during the global financial crisis between Sep 2008 and Jun 2009. They divided each time series into plunging stage, fluctuating stage, and soaring stage. They unveiled power-law tails in the recurrence distributions and the exponents $\delta(Q)$ are decreasing functions. Moreover, the power-law tail exponent is the lowest in the plunging stage for various types of markets, and increases monotonically from the plunging stage to the soaring stage in emerging markets.

5.1.2 Stretched Exponential Distribution

Wang et al. (2006) investigated the 10-min volatility time series of the Standard and Poor's 500 index from January 1, 1984, to December 31, 1996, and the 1-min volatility time series of the 30 stocks that form the Dow Jones Industrial index from January 1, 2001, to December 31, 2002. In their study, they did not use the volatility directly, rather they removed the intraday pattern. They found that the scaled distributions $\langle\tau\rangle p_Q(\tau)$ collapse to a single curve $f(\tau/\langle\tau\rangle)$ with respect to $\tau/\langle\tau\rangle$, and the scaling function $f(\tau/\langle\tau\rangle)$ follows a stretched exponential form $f(\tau/\langle\tau\rangle) \sim \exp[-a(\tau/\langle\tau\rangle)^\gamma]$. The scaling relation with $\gamma = 0.38 \pm 0.05$ and $a = 3.9 \pm 0.5$ seems to hold for a wide range of the threshold Q, for all the time series investigated, and for timescales Δt ranging from 1 min to 30 min. The main conclusions have been validated by F. Wang et al. (2007) using the 1-min prices of the 30 DJIA constituent stocks from January 2, 2001, to December 31, 2002, the 10-min S&P 500 index prices from January 2, 1984, to December 31, 1996, the daily prices of more than 6000 US stocks, the daily exchange rates of 35 other currencies to the United States Dollar (USD) from 1971 to 2006, the daily spot prices of West Texas Intermediate (WTI) crude oil since 30 December 1985, and the daily gold prices (London P.M.) since January 2, 1985. Jung et al. (2008) also validated these results on the daily data of three representative Japanese stocks from 1977 to 2004 and the 1-min data of 1817 stocks from January 1997 to December 1997 listed on the Tokyo Stock Exchange. They further confirmed the results by performing one-sample KS tests for the stretched exponential distributions and two-sample KS tests for the scaling relation.

Wang et al. (2008) (received July 30, 2007; published January 29, 2008) investigated the 1-min volatility time series of 500 constituent stocks of the S&P 500 index from January 1, 2001, to December 31, 2002. They found that the recurrence intervals follow the stretched exponential distribution and the moments analysis shows that the distributions exhibit multiscaling behavior. Wang et al. (2009) further investigated the 1-min volatility series of 1137 most traded U.S. stocks for the two-year period 2001–2002. They applied the stretched exponential to fit the recurrence interval distribution and found that the exponent γ depends on the threshold in the range between $Q = 1$ and 6, which depends on the capitalization, risk, and return but almost does not depend on the number of trades. The moments analysis confirms the multiscaling behavior.

With the KS test, Ren and Zhou (2008) reported multiscaling behavior in the recurrence intervals of the 1-min volatility of the Shanghai Stock Exchange Composite Index (SSEC) and the Shenzhen Stock Exchange Composite Index

(SZCI) from January 2004 to June 2006, and the distributions have a stretched exponential form where the parameter γ decreases with increasing Q. However, for the 1-min time series of realized SSEC volatility defined by the sum of absolute higher-frequency intraday returns, Ren et al. (2009) reported a scaling behavior based on the KS test. For the 5-min volatility time series of the SSEC from February 28, 2001, to April 17, 2006, Zhang et al. (2010) argued that, for the 5-min SSEC volatility, the recurrence interval distributions have a scaling behavior in the form of stretched exponential.

Qiu et al. (2008) analyzed the 1-min volatility of four high liquid Chinese stocks covering three entire years from 2004 to 2006 and reported stretched exponential distributions of the recurrence intervals that show scaling behavior. Ren et al. (2009) considered the 1-min volatility series of thirty liquid Chinese stocks from January 2004 to June 2006. The KS test shows that twelve stocks exhibit scaling behaviors in the distributions of τ. Furthermore, the KS test and weighted KS test show that the scaled return interval distributions of six stocks (out of the twelve stocks) can be nicely fitted by a stretched exponential function with $\gamma \approx 0.31$. Ren et al. (2009) investigated the 1-min realized volatility series of twenty-two constituent stocks of SSEC from January 2004 to June 2006. KS tests show that the recurrence interval distribution for the realized volatility shows a better scaling behavior than the absolute returns and the scaling function for eight stocks could be fitted by a stretched exponential distribution.

Jeon et al. (2010) investigated the daily volatility series of four Korean stocks from January 1993 to December 2007. KS tests suggest the presence of multiscaling behavior and deny that the recurrence interval distributions are stretched exponential.

Xie et al. (2014) investigated the recurrence intervals of the daily volatility time series of four energy futures traded on the New York Mercantile Exchange (NYMEX). They found that the recurrence interval distributions decay as a stretched exponential, where the exponent β decreases with increasing threshold Q, and there is no scaling behavior in the distributions. These findings were validated by the KS test and the CvM test.

Jiang et al. (2016) performed an extensive investigation of the 1-min volatility time series of 1820 Chinese stocks. They compared the stretched exponential distribution in Eq. (2.15), the power-law distribution with an exponential cutoff in Eq. (2.7), the q-exponential distribution in Eq. (2.11), and the Weibull distribution in Eq. (2.13). Statistical tests showed that these stocks do not exhibit a scaling behavior in their recurrence interval distributions and the stretched exponential distribution performs the best, especially for large thresholds.

5.1.3 Weibull

Zhou et al. (2016) investigated the recurrence intervals of 17 daily futures volatility time series in the Chinese commodity futures market. They argued that, for each asset, the recurrence interval distributions have a scaling behavior for different thresholds Q. The KS test showed that the distributions can be well fitted by a Weibull instead of a power law.

Zhou et al. (2020) studied the 1-min volatility time series of the CSI 300 futures from April 16, 2010, to August 31, 2015. The KS tests suggest that the recurrence interval distribution is better fitted by a Weibull than a power law.

5.1.4 q-Weibull Distribution

Reboredo et al. (2014) performed a nonstandard recurrence interval analysis on the intraday returns for the S&P 500, DAX, and IBEX-35 indexes. They did not vary the threshold Q but used the Hill estimator to determine the threshold that is adopted to identify extreme returns. With the χ^2 tests and the KS tests, they found that the recurrence intervals between absolute extreme returns are well characterized by the q-Weibull distribution. On the contrary, the q-exponential distribution, the Weibull distribution, the exponential distribution, and the gamma distribution are rejected.

5.1.5 Memory Effects

Yamasaki et al. (2005) investigated memory effects in the recurrence intervals of daily volatility records of seven stocks and seven currencies. For each Q and volatility time series, they sorted the set of return intervals in increasing order and divided it into eight subsets of the same size. They found that, for each subset, the scaled conditional probability distributions $\langle \tau \rangle p_Q(\tau | \tau_0)$ collapse onto a single scaling function. However, the scaling functions are different for different subsets. The mean recurrence interval $\langle \tau | \tau_0 \rangle$ is found to be an increasing function of τ_0, showing that short recurrence intervals tend to be followed by short ones, and long recurrence intervals tend to be followed by long ones. In addition, detrended fluctuation analysis of the recurrence interval time series unveiled long-range correlations in the recurrence interval time series.

Using the 10-min volatility time series of the S&P 500 index from January 1, 1984, to December 31, 1996, and the 1-min volatility time series of the 30 stocks that form the Dow Jones Industrial index from January 1, 2001, to December 31, 2002, Wang et al. (2006) investigated scaled conditional distributions $\langle \tau \rangle p_Q(\tau | \tau_0)$ and found qualitatively similar results. They also found that the mean conditional recurrence interval $\langle \tau | \tau_0 \rangle$ increases linearly with τ_0.

The clustered interval analysis also showed that $\langle \tau | \tau_0 \rangle$ is an increasing function of the cluster size n for recurrence intervals above the median of the entire interval records and a decreasing function of the cluster size n for recurrence intervals below the median of the entire interval records. The detrended fluctuation analysis unveiled a crossover phenomenon and long-range correlations at both small and large sales. Wang et al. (2007) validated these results with more assets.

Actually, to the best of our knowledge, both short-term memory and long-term correlations have been confirmed in all the recurrence interval analyses that investigate the memory effects. Related financial assets include the daily volatility of three stocks from 1977 to 2004 and the 1-min data of 1817 stocks from January 1997 to December 1997 listed on the Tokyo Stock Exchange (Jung et al., 2008), the daily volatility of 4 NYMEX energy futures (Xie et al., 2014), the daily volatility of the WTI and Brent spot prices from May 20, 1987, to September 18, 2012 (Yuan et al., 2014), the 1-min volatility time series of 10 stock indexes during the plunging stage, fluctuating stage and soaring stage of the global financial crisis between September 2008 and June 2009 (Li & Liaw, 2015), 17 daily futures volatility time series in the Chinese commodity futures market (Zhou et al., 2016), and the 1-min data of the CSI 300 futures from April 16, 2010, to August 31, 2015 (Zhou et al., 2020).

Interestingly, Weber, Wang, Vodenska-Chitkushev, Havlin, and Stanley (2007) studied the impact of the Omori law on the memory effects in volatility recurrence intervals and showed that a significant amount of short-term and long-term memory is induced by these crashes and subcrashes on different scales.

Meng et al. (2012) further confirmed the presence of multifractal nature in the recurrence interval time series based on an artificial market. Such multifractal behavior has also been observed in other markets, such as the 5-min volatility time series of the SSEC index from December 1, 2006, to June 1, 2012 (Deng & Wang, 2015; Dong & Wang, 2013), the 5-min data of the SZSE index from 1 December 2006 to 1 June 2012 (Deng & Wang, 2015; Yang & Wang, 2016), and the 1-min data of the CSI 300 futures from April 16, 2010, to August 31, 2015 (Zhou et al., 2020).

5.2 Financial Returns

5.2.1 Power-law Distribution

Yamasaki et al. (2006) performed recurrence interval analysis on daily returns with negative thresholds Q. In the return time series of the stocks of IBM, DoPond, and Kodak, the exchange rates of US-Japan, US-Switzerland, and

US-Sweden, and federal fund, gold and oil, they found that the curves of the scaled distributions $p_Q(\tau)\langle\tau\rangle$ against the scaled recurrence intervals $\tau/\langle\tau\rangle$ from different $Q \in [-1.0, -1.5, -2.5, -3.0]$ collapse onto a single curve, which is a universal function. They further found that

$$\frac{\langle\tau|\tau_0\rangle}{\langle\tau\rangle} = \left(\frac{\tau_0}{\langle\tau\rangle}\right)^{0.25}. \tag{5.5}$$

Bogachev et al. (2007) analyzed the daily returns of several stocks (IBM, GM, GE, Boeing, etc.), exchange rates versus U.S. dollar (DM, AUS dollar, and CAN dollar), crude oil prices (Brent and WTI), and stock market indices (Dow Jones and S&P 500) and found that the recurrence intervals for positive thresholds of the return time series are distributed as a power law. However, they found no evidence of scaling behavior and the observed quantities depend both on the threshold Q and system size. They argued that the deviations from the power-law distribution at smaller return intervals are caused by the finite-size effect. They also confirmed the power-law relationship in Eq. (5.5) but did not report the exponent due to less statistics caused by the fact that the time series are short. By studying a variety of representative financial records (market indices, stock prices, exchange rates, and commodities), Bogachev and Bunde (2008) confirmed these findings for both positive and negative thresholds.

Ren and Zhou (2010) investigated the probability distributions of the recurrence intervals for positive and negative thresholds using the 1-min returns of two indices and 20 stocks in China's stock market. They found that the distributions of recurrence intervals for positive and negative thresholds are symmetric, and display power-law tails, which are confirmed by three goodness-of-fit measures, including the Kolmogorov–Smirnov (KS) statistic, the weighted KS statistic and the Cramér–von Mises criterion. They also observed long-term and short-term memory effects in the recurrence intervals for positive and negative thresholds. They discovered a modified power-law relationship between $\langle\tau|\tau_0\rangle$ and τ_0, as expressed in Eq. (4.15).

5.2.2 q-Weibull Distribution

Reboredo et al. (2014) performed a nonstandard recurrence interval analysis on the intraday returns for the S&P 500, DAX, and IBEX-35 indexes. They did not vary the threshold Q but used the Hill estimator to determine the threshold that is adopted to identify extreme returns. With the χ^2 tests and the KS tests, they found that the recurrence intervals between different kinds of extreme returns are well characterized by the q-Weibull distribution. On the contrary, the q-exponential distribution, the Weibull distribution, the exponential distribution, and the gamma distribution are rejected.

5.2.3 Stretched Exponential Distribution

Suo, Wang, and Li (2015) considered the 1-min return time series for the spot and futures prices of the China Securities Index 300 (CSI 300) stock index from April 16, 2010, to December 31, 2012. They found that the recurrence intervals for $|Q| \in [1.0, 1.8]$ have a stretched exponential distribution and argued that there is a scaling behavior in the distributions. They further confirmed that the recurrence interval time series possess short-term and long-term correlations.

Zhang et al. (2018) investigated the 1-min return time series of the fuel oil futures listed on the Shanghai Futures Exchange from January 1, 2015, to December 30, 2016. They also reported a stretched exponential distribution, which does not show scaling behavior. They also confirmed that the recurrence interval time series possess short-term and long-term correlations.

5.2.4 q-exponential Distribution

Ludescher et al. (2011) considered the daily returns of sixteen representative financial records (stocks, indices, commodities, and exchange rates) and studied the recurrence interval distribution for negative thresholds. They found that the distributions can be best fitted by a q-exponential, as expressed in Eq. (2.11), and the parameter q depends on the mean recurrence interval:

$$q = 1 + q_0 \ln (\langle \tau \rangle / 2), \tag{5.6}$$

where $q_0 = 0.168$. When $\langle \tau \rangle \to 2$, we have $q \to 1$ and the q-exponential shrinks to an exponential. Although the distribution $p_Q(\tau; \Phi)$ depends on Q, it is universal over different assets for fixed thresholds. Moreover, Ludescher and Bunde (2014) found that $p_Q(\tau; \Phi)$ is independent of the time scale Δt used for the definition of returns, where the returns are detrended by the volatility.

With the daily return time series of five stock market indices (S&P 500, KOSPI 200, CAC 40, DAX 30, and SMI 20), Chicheportiche and Chakraborti (2014) found that the recurrence interval distributions do not fit power laws but can be well fitted by q-exponentials, and confirmed the logarithmic dependence between q and $\langle \tau \rangle$.

Jiang et al. (2018) analyzed the daily returns of the Dow Jones Industrial Average (DJIA) index from February 16, 1885, to December 31, 2015. They adopted the maximum likelihood estimation to fit the recurrence intervals to three distributions (stretched exponential, q-exponential, and Weibull). Since each distribution has only one parameter after normalization, a comparison of the likelihoods favors the q-exponential distribution. No scaling behavior was found in the distributions since the parameters change with Q.

Li et al. (2022) performed the same analysis on the daily returns of the Shanghai Stock Exchange Composite (SSEC) index from January 1, 1997, to December 31, 2019 and the WTI Crude Oil Prices (WTI) price from March 31, 1983, to December 31, 2019, and the DJIA index from February 16, 1885, to December 31, 2019 and confirmed that the q-exponential is the best distribution for the recurrence intervals.

5.3 Trading Volume

Besides the prices of assets, trading volumes are another important building block for modeling asset markets since trading volumes reflect the trading activity of market practitioners. There are a variety of measures for trading activity. Lo and Wang (2000) found that two mutual-fund separation theorems, the capital asset pricing model (CAPM) and the intertemporal CAPM (ICAPM), suggest that share turnover is a natural definition for trading activity. However, the raw trading volumes are usually utilized in the recurrence interval analysis. There are also studies investigating the absolute logarithmic changes of trading volumes.

5.3.1 Trading Volume Per Se

Consider a trading volume time series $\{V(t), \cdots, V(T)\}$. The trading volumes are usually normalized before further analysis by dividing their standard deviation

$$\frac{V(t)}{\sqrt{\langle V^2(t)\rangle - \langle V(t)\rangle^2}} \to V(t). \tag{5.7}$$

After normalization, the recurrence intervals are comparable for different assets. Since trading volumes are positive, we can also normalize $V(t)$ using $\sqrt{\langle V^2(t)\rangle}$ or $\langle V(t)\rangle$.

For intraday high-frequency trading volumes, there is a U-shaped intraday pattern (Vodenska-Chitkushev et al., 2008; Wang et al., 2007, 2006, 2008), which can be calculated as follows:

$$A(s) = \frac{1}{T}\sum_{t=1}^{T} V_t(s), \tag{5.8}$$

which is the average volume at a specific time moment s of the trading day averaged over all T trading days and $V_i(s)$ is the trading volume at moment s of day t. We then remove the intraday pattern from the raw trading volume time series:

$$\frac{V(t)}{A(s)} \to V(t). \tag{5.9}$$

Then the normalization operation in Eq. (5.7) is applied.

Ren and Zhou (2010) studied the statistical properties of the recurrence intervals of the 1-min intraday data of 20 liquid Chinese stocks from January 2000 to May 2009 and two Chinese indices from January 2003 to April 2009. They found that the tail of the recurrence interval distribution follows a power-law scaling. Analysis of the scaled conditional distributions $\langle\tau\rangle p_Q(\tau|\tau_0)$ with respect to the scale recurrence intervals $\tau/\langle\tau\rangle$ and the scaled mean conditional recurrence intervals with respect to the scale recurrence intervals $\tau_0/\langle\tau\rangle$ confirmed the presence of short-term memory, while the detrended fluctuation analysis revealed strong long-range correlations in the recurrence interval time series.

Zhou et al. (2020) performed recurrence interval analysis on the 1-min trading volume time series of the CSI 300 futures from April 16, 2010, to August 31, 2015. The KS tests suggested that the recurrence interval distribution is better fitted by a Weibull than a power law. Their study also confirmed the presence of short memory, long memory, and multifractal nature in the recurrence interval time series.

5.3.2 Volatility of Trading Volume

Podobnik et al. (2009) defined the volume volatility through the logarithmic change in trading volume:

$$R_V(t) = \ln V(t) - \ln V(t-1), \tag{5.10}$$

such that the volume volatility is

$$v(t) = |R_V(t)|, \tag{5.11}$$

which is further normalized by the standard deviation:

$$\frac{v(t)}{\sqrt{\langle v^2(t)\rangle - \langle v(t)\rangle^2}} \rightarrow v(t). \tag{5.12}$$

We can also normalize $v(t)$ using $\sqrt{\langle v^2(t)\rangle}$ or $\langle v(t)\rangle$.

Li et al. (2011) studied the daily trading volume volatility of 17197 stocks in the US stock markets from January 1, 1989, to December 31, 2008. They find that the recurrence intervals of volume volatility have a power-law scaling for different Q. However, the exponent α differs for different stocks. It is found that α decreases with the increasing of the stock lifetime, market capitalization, volume, and trading value. Analysis of the scaled conditional distributions $\langle\tau\rangle p_Q(\tau|\tau_0)$ with respect to the scale recurrence intervals $\tau/\langle\tau\rangle$ and the scaled mean conditional recurrence intervals with respect to the scale recurrence intervals $\tau_0/\langle\tau\rangle$ confirmed the presence of short-term memory, while the detrended fluctuation analysis revealed strong long-range correlations in the recurrence interval time series.

Wu et al. (2014) performed similar analysis on 2282 stocks in the Chinese market and confirmed the scaling behavior in the power-law distributions. They found that the power-law scaling exponent α decreases with the increase of stock lifetime, but does not depend on market capitalization, mean volume, and mean trading value.

Ouyang et al. (2014) introduced a slightly different definition for volume volatility:

$$v(t) = \frac{|R_V(t) - \langle R_V \rangle|}{\sqrt{\langle R_V^2 \rangle - \langle R_V \rangle^2}}.$$ (5.13)

They investigated the daily volume volatility of 259 stocks each for the Shanghai, Shenzhen, Taiwan, and Hong Kong stock markets. For each market, the recurrence intervals of all 259 stocks were obtained and put together as one sample for analysis. They found power-law distributions with the exponents being α = 4.2 for Shanghai, 4.3 for Shenzhen, 4.7 for Taiwan, and 3.7 for Hong Kong.

5.4 Risk Estimation

5.4.1 Mean Recurrence Interval, Loss Probability, and VaR

As shown in Section 4.1, in the Value at Risk analysis, the relation between the mean recurrence interval $\langle \tau \rangle$ and the threshold Q has important implications. A variety of studies have investigated this relationship.

Yamasaki et al. (2006) considered the daily returns with negative thresholds Q of the stocks of IBM, DoPond, and Kodak, the exchange rates of US-Japan, US-Switzerland, and US-Sweden, and federal fund, gold and oil. They found the power-law dependence between the mean recurrence interval $\langle \tau \rangle$ and the associated threshold Q:

$$\langle \tau \rangle \sim Q^\beta$$ (5.14)

with $\beta = 3.3$.

Podobnik et al. (2009) investigated the daily trading volume volatility of the Standard and Poor's (S&P) 500 Index from January 1950 to July 2009, 1819 New York Stock Exchange (NYSE) constituent stocks till July 17, 2009, and twenty-eight worldwide financial indices. They derived and empirically validated the power-law dependence expressed in Eq. (5.14). This power-law relationship also holds for five different levels of financial aggregation, including Europe, Asia, North and South America, the world without the United States, and the entire world.

There are other studies conforming Eq. (5.14). For instance, Ren and Zhou (2010) found that β is close to 3 for the 1-min return time series of two indices and four stocks in the Chinese stock market, He and Chen (2011) found that $\beta = 2.7655 \pm 0.0775$ for the daily volatility of WTI and $\beta = 2.6864 \pm 0.0419$ for the daily volatility of Brent, Suo et al. (2015) found that $\beta = 0.33$ for the 1-min return time series of the CSI 300 index futures prices and $\beta = 2.6$ for the 1-min return time series of the CSI 300 index spot prices, and Zhou et al. (2020) found that $\beta = 2.53$ for the 1-min CSI 300 futures volatility and $\beta = 2.55$ for the 1-min CSI 300 futures volume volatility.

However, Zhang et al. (2018) did not find the power-law dependence in the 1-min return time series from January 1, 2015, to December 30, 2016, of the fuel oil futures listed on the Shanghai Futures Exchange.

Bogachev and Bunde (2009a) showed that the Bogachev-Bunde method provides much better estimation of the Value at Risk as illustrated by three representative financial assets (DJIA, IBM, and GBP), where the recurrence intervals are distributed as a power law. Ludescher et al. (2011) applied the Bogachev-Bunde method for IBM, where the q-exponential distribution is used to model the recurrence intervals.

Ren and Zhou (2010) calculated the empirical and theoretical conditional loss probabilities $p^*_{|\tau_0}$ of two indices and four stocks in the Chinese stock market and found comparative results.

5.4.2 Hazard Probability

Bogachev et al. (2007) provided the analytic expression of the hazard probability $W_{PL}(\Delta|t)$ shown in Eq. (4.55) for the synthetic time series generated according to the multifractal random cascade (MRC) model (see Section 5.5.2 for details), where the recurrence interval distribution decays approximately by a power law with the tail exponent $0 < \delta < 1$ being a decreasing function of Q.

Bogachev and Bunde (2009a) observed finite-size effects in $W_{PL}(\Delta|t)$ and proposed the following ansatz:

$$W_{PL}(\Delta|t) = \frac{\delta\Delta t}{t + \delta\Delta t}, \qquad (5.15)$$

which fits the curves better. They found that the $W(1|t)$ functions of the negative price returns of financial records agree with those of the MRC data. In addition, they found that the recurrence interval analysis has comparative predictive performance as the conventional precursory pattern recognition technique (PRT) for the MRC data. However, the RIA method outperforms the PRT method in predicting extreme events for financial records. In contrast, for monofractal time series, the PRT outperforms the RIA (Bogachev & Bunde, 2011). When there is additive white noise in the raw time series with low and intermediate noise-to-signal ratios, the RIA is found to predict considerably better than the PRT (Bogachev & Bunde, 2011).

The agreement between "theoretical" and empirical hazard functions has been reported for many financial time series, such as the 1-min returns of two indices and four stocks in the Chinese stock market (Ren & Zhou, 2010), the daily volatility time series of four NYMEX energy futures (Xie et al., 2014), the 1-min return time series of the CSI 300 spot and futures prices (Suo et al., 2015), the 1-min volatility time series of 1820 Chinese stocks (Jiang et al., 2016), the daily returns of the DJIA index (Jiang et al., 2018), and the 1-min return time series of the fuel oil futures listed on the Shanghai Futures Exchange (Zhang et al., 2018).

5.5 Simulational and Theoretical Analyses

5.5.1 Time Series with Linear Long-term Correlations

The autocorrelation function $C(s)$ of a long-term correlated time series $\{x(i)\}$ decays asymptotically as a power law of the time scale s:

$$C(s) \sim s^{-\gamma}, \quad 0 < \gamma < 1. \tag{5.16}$$

where γ is the correlation exponent.

Bunde et al. (2003) and Bunde et al. (2005) numerically studied the recurrence interval distributions of long-term correlated time series. They found that the recurrence intervals follow a stretched exponential with the exponent very close to γ. The recurrence intervals are also long-term correlated with the correlation exponent $2(1 - H)$ close to γ. Altmann and Kantz (2005) verified numerically the stretched exponential distribution for long-term correlated time series and pointed out that it is restricted to linear long-term correlations.

Eichner et al. (2007) performed an extensive investigation of long-term correlated time series with four probability densities (Gaussian, exponential, power law, and log normal) and various correlation exponents γ. They found that the recurrence intervals are distributed as a power law for small intervals due to the discretization effects and as a stretched exponential for large intervals:

$$\langle\tau\rangle p(\tau) \sim \begin{cases} \left(\frac{\tau}{\langle\tau\rangle}\right)^{\gamma'-1} & \text{for } 1 \ll \tau \leq \langle\tau\rangle, \\ \exp\left[-\left(b\frac{\tau}{\langle\tau\rangle}\right)^{\gamma'}\right] & \text{for } \langle\tau\rangle < \tau \ll T, \end{cases} \tag{5.17}$$

where T is the size of the raw time series. Very importantly, they observed finite-size effects in the recurrence interval distributions for large thresholds Q. In contrast, Moloney and Davidsen's (2009) numerical simulations showed significant deviations from the power law for small recurrence intervals and from the stretched exponential for large recurrence intervals, and the deviations are more profound for higher thresholds.

For synthetic $1/f$ noises that are long-term correlated with $\gamma = 1$, Blender et al. (2008) found that the recurrence interval distribution can be well fitted by a Weibull distribution, while the stretched exponential fit and the power-law fit are much worse.

Zhao et al. (2016) investigated the ARFIMA processes and found, for long-term correlated time series, that the recurrence intervals are distributed as a stretched exponential and possess long-term correlations. Interestingly, they found that, for anti-persistent time series, the recurrence intervals are exponentially distributed and do not have long-term correlations.

There are also theoretical studies. Olla (2007) provided an analytical study of the recurrence interval distribution for linear long-term correlated time series based on an ϵ expansion in the correlation exponent

$$C(s) = As^{-(1-\epsilon)}, \ 0 \le \epsilon < 1 \tag{5.18}$$

and obtained that

$$C(\tau) = \Pr(T < \tau) \sim 1 - \exp\left[-\frac{2\epsilon}{AQ^2}\tau^{1-\epsilon}\right], \tag{5.19}$$

which is the Weibull distribution instead of the stretched exponential distribution called by Olla (2007). Note that the distribution depends on the threshold Q. Santhanam and Kantz (2008) also derived the Weibull distribution using a different method, which does not depend on Q and holds good for large mean recurrence intervals.

5.5.2 Time Series with Nonlinear Correlations

Bogachev et al. (2007) studied the effect of nonlinear correlations on the recurrence interval distributions in synthetic multifractal time series generated from the multiplicative random cascade (MRC) process with vanishing linear correlations characterized by the zero mean of the random multipliers. They found that the recurrence interval distribution exhibits a power-law decay whose exponent varies with the threshold Q and the recurrence interval time series possess long-term correlations. Bogachev (2008a, 2008b) further obtained similar results for MRC time series with linear long-term correlations introduced by the nonzero mean of the random multipliers.

Bogachev and Bunde (2008) verified these findings for the multifractal random walks (MRWs) introduced by Bacry et al. (2001) that also have vanishing linear correlations.

Ludescher and Bunde (2014) considered three market models: MRC, MRW, and GARCH(1,1). They found that the recurrence intervals of the GARCH(1,1) time series cannot be well fitted by any distributions we mentioned in this Element caused by the fact that these returns are only short-term correlated, the recurrence intervals of the MRC time series are power-law distributed, and the recurrence intervals of the MRW time series are distributed according to the q-exponential.

We must stress that the results of Bogachev and Bunde (2008) and Ludescher and Bunde (2014) are not contradictory for the MRW time series. Bogachev and Bunde (2008) focused on recurrence intervals that are not too small (see Fig. 5(b) therein), while Ludescher and Bunde (2014) investigated all the recurrence intervals (see Fig. 7 therein).

5.6 Microscopic Models

5.6.1 Order-driven Model

In order to understand the microscopic mechanisms of the statistical properties of the recurrence intervals of financial returns, Meng et al. (2012) adopted Gu and Zhou's (2009) order-driven model, which is an improved version of Mike and Farmer's (2008) empirical behavioral model. There are two adjustable parameters in Gu and Zhou's (2009) model: the Hurst exponents H_x and H_s of the relative prices x and directions s of the submitted orders. Gu and Zhou (2009) found that the recurrence intervals of ultra-high-frequency returns can be well fitted by a generalized Gamma function that is independent of Q:

$$p\left(\frac{\tau}{\langle\tau\rangle}\right) = A\left(\frac{\tau}{\langle\tau\rangle}\right)^{-\delta} \exp\left[-b\left(\frac{\tau}{\langle\tau\rangle}\right)^{\gamma}\right],$$ (5.20)

where δ, γ, and b are parameters and

$$A = \delta/\gamma^{\frac{\beta-1}{\delta}}\Gamma((1-\beta)/\delta)$$ (5.21)

is the normalization factor. They found that the generalized Gamma distribution performs better than the Weibull distribution. They also found that the power-law exponent δ is an increasing function of H_x. In addition, stronger linear correlations in the relative prices (i.e., larger H_x) result in stronger long-term correlations and multifractal strength in the recurrence interval time series.

5.6.2 Agent-based Models

There are also agent-based models showing that the recurrence interval time series of volatility exhibit multifractal nature, such as the model of Dong and Wang (2013) based on the percolation system on the Sierpinski carpet lattice and the model of Deng and Wang (2015) (see also Pei and Wang (2015)) based on the oriented percolation system on square lattice.

Gontis (2016) and Gontis et al. (2016) derived macroscopic equations based on the microscopic herding interactions of agents and reported that they were able to reproduce the power-law distributions of recurrence intervals in high-frequency return time series.

6 Final Remarks

6.1 Brief Summary

As surveyed in Section 5, there are a variety of empirical studies on the recurrence interval distributions of low- and high-frequency volatility, return, and trading volume time series. Different distributions have been proposed for the partial or entire sample. However, only a small part of these studies included statistical tests. We recommend the stretched distribution for volatility time series, the q-exponential distribution for return time series, and the power-law tailed distribution for trading volume time series. We note that studies on trading volume are the least numerous.

We note that the candidate distribution functions presented in Section 2.2 do not contain a left-side cutoff u, which is however very important in practical applications. In other words, a more suitable expression of distribution $p(\tau)$ should be the following:

$$p_u(\tau) = \begin{cases} p(\tau) & \text{if } \tau \geqslant u > 0 \\ 0 & \text{if } \tau < u. \end{cases} \tag{6.1}$$

In this situation, it has been shown that there is a natural nestedness between power laws and stretched exponential (and Weibull which is close) such that calibrations with power laws and stretched exponentials can be indistinguishable in essence (Malevergne et al., 2005; Malevergne & Sornette, 2006). This deep insight explains why empirical studies have used different distributions with some success. In many cases, the same generic large class of distributions have been adopted that are deeply related to each other.

On the contrary, the presence of short- and long-term memory effects in recurrence interval time series is well established through empirical investigations. There are also studies reporting the presence of multifractality, which is however not confirmed by statistical tests.

6.2 Other Financial variables

The recurrence interval analysis has been utilized to study the time series of returns, volatility, and trading volumes of financial assets. There are other important financial variables that can be studied, especially those related to liquidity. For instance, the illiquidity measure (Amihud, 2002), the bid-ask spread, and order book depth are important in quantifying the stability of markets.

6.3 Copulas

Chicheportiche and Chakraborti (2014) proposed that n-points copulas provide a model-free mathematical framework to study recurrence intervals. With the daily negative returns of the IBM stock from 1962 to 2010, Chicheportiche and Chakraborti (2017) further illustrated that no scaling occurs when there are nonlinear correlations and/or several time scales in the dependence structure of the raw time series. Therefore, copulas are helpful for distinguishing between scaling and multiscaling behaviors.

Recently, Li et al. (2022) proposed a RIA-EVT-Copula framework for the prediction of extreme events by considering the correlations between the recurrence intervals and the corresponding sizes of extremes above the thresholds (exceeding sizes). Their in-sample and out-of-sample tests revealed that the RIA-EVT-Copula framework provides better prediction performance than the conventional model based on the hazard probability without considering the interaction between recurrence intervals and exceeding sizes. We argue that this new framework can be applied in future studies.

6.4 Autoregressive Conditional Recurrence Interval Models

The univariate and multivariate autoregressive conditional recurrence interval models were proposed by Dai et al. (2018). This new class of models has not been applied to the analysis of financial time series for risk management and extreme event forecasting.

6.5 Expected Hazard Time

6.5.1 Expected Hazard Time

The expected hazard time is the expected time until the next event conditional of a time t elapsed since the last event, which can be calculated if the recurrence interval distribution $p(t)$ is known (Sornette & Knopoff, 1997):

$$\langle \Delta t \rangle = \frac{\int_t^\infty (u-t)p(u)\mathrm{d}u}{\int_t^\infty p(t)\mathrm{d}t}. \tag{6.2}$$

Apparently, $\langle \Delta t \rangle$ is a function of t. Sornette and Knopoff (1997) studied the dependence of $\langle \Delta t \rangle$ on t for quite a few distributions, who have presented an intuitive and full classification of the different regimes, depending on whether the tail of the unconditional distribution is thinner or fatter than the exponential law. To the best of our knowledge, this quantity has not been well studied in econophysics.

6.5.2 Expected Conditional Hazard Time

As a generalization of the conditional mean recurrence interval $\langle \tau | \tau_0 \rangle$, (Livina et al., 2005; Livina, Tuzov, et al., 2005) introduced the expected residual time:

$$\langle \Delta t | \tau_0 \rangle = \frac{\int_t^\infty (u - t) p(u|\tau_0)\mathrm{d}u}{\int_t^\infty p(t|\tau_0)\mathrm{d}t}, \tag{6.3}$$

which is conditional on the preceding recurrence interval being τ_0. We can certainly call it "the expected conditional hazard time." If $t = 0$, it is simple to demonstrate that the expected conditional residual time is the same as $\langle \tau | \tau_0 \rangle$.

The expected conditional hazard time considers whether $\langle \Delta t \rangle$ depends on τ_0, or equivalently, whether $\langle \Delta t \rangle = \langle \Delta t | \tau_0 \rangle$. If $p(u|\tau_0)$ does not depend on τ_0, that is, $p(u|\tau_0) = p(u)$, then $\langle \Delta t \rangle = \langle \Delta t | \tau_0 \rangle$. However, most empirical studies have shown that $p(u|\tau_0)$ does depend on τ_0. Hence, the expected conditional hazard time would improve the estimation of risks.

6.6 Limitations

Recurrence intervals are a kind of two-point statistics of the full information embedded in a series of event occurrence times $t \in \{t_1, \cdots, t_n\}$ from which the recurrence intervals $\tau_n := t_n - t_{n-1}$ are defined, where t_i is the time when the i-th event occurs. As a natural generalization, besides $j = 1$, we can look at $t_n - t_{n-i}$ for arbitrary $i \in \mathbb{N}$. Indeed, the full analysis should be in terms of all multiple-point statistics of the joint distributions of all the t_n's. We can thus look at more complex information involving three times (t_{n-1}, t_n, and t_{n+1}), four times, and so forth.

Hence, recurrence intervals are a poor representation of the full richness of time series and the RIA approach is actually a very strong reduction of information. This has been demonstrated by Saichev and Sornette (2006, 2007) for earthquake recurrence intervals based on the epidemic-type aftershock sequence (ETAS) model (a Hawkes self-excited conditional point process) (see Helmstetter & Sornette, 2002a, 2002b, and references therein), which has not been investigated for financial time series. Such point processes are important in modelling financial time series, which often arrives at remarkably richer results. For instance, Wehrli and Sornette (2022) used a peak-over-threshold analysis of returns to successfully explain the long-lasting excess volatility puzzle of Shiller (1981) for the first time.

Overall, the recurrence interval analysis is a phenomenological analysis, which does not dig into the deeper underlying mechanisms that generate the investigated time series. Point-process rate models such as Hawkes models are more promising tools in analyzing financial time series.

References

Alessi, L., & Detken, C. (2011). Quasi real time early warning indicators for costly asset price boom/bust cycles: A role for global liquidity. *Eur. J. Polit. Econ.*, *27*, 520–533. https://doi.org/10.1016/j.ejpoleco.2011.01.003.

Alessio, E., Carbone, A., Castelli, G., & Frappietro, V. (2002). Second-order moving average and scaling of stochastic time series. *Eur. Phys. J. B*, *27*(2), 197–200. https://doi.org/10.1140/epjb/e20020150.

Altmann, E. G., & Kantz, H. (2005). Recurrence time analysis, long-term correlations, and extreme events. *Phys. Rev. E*, *71*, 056106. https://doi.org/10.1103/PhysRevE.71.056106.

Amihud, Y. (2002). Illiquidity and stock returns: Cross-section and time-series effects. *J. Financ. Markets*, *5*, 31–56. https://doi.org/10.1016/S1386-4181(01)00024-6.

Anderson, T. W., & Darling, D. A. (1952). Asymptotic theory of certain "goodness of fit" criteria based on stochastic processes. *Ann. Math. Statist.*, *23*(2), 193–212. https://doi.org/10.1214/aoms/1177729437.

Arianos, S., & Carbone, A. (2007). Detrending moving average algorithm: A closed-form approximation of the scaling law. *Physica A*, *382*(1), 9–15. https://doi.org/10.1016/j.physa.2007.02.074.

Audit, B., Bacry, E., Muzy, J.- F., & Arnéodo, A. (2002). Wavelet-based estimators of scaling behavior. *IEEE Trans. Info. Theory*, *48*(11), 2938–2954. https://doi.org/10.1109/TIT.2002.802631.

Babecký, J., Havránek, T., Matějů, J., Rusnák, M., Šmídková, K., & Vašíček, B. (2014). Banking, debt, and currency crises in developed countries: Stylized facts and early warning indicators. *J. Financ. Stabil.*, *15*, 1–17. https://doi.org/10.1016/j.jfs.2014.07.001.

Bacry, E., Delour, J., & Muzy, J.- F. (2001). Multifractal random walk. *Phys. Rev. E*, *64*(2), 026103. https://.org/10.1103/PhysRevE.64.026103.

Bagnato, L., De Capitani, L., & Punzo, A. (2017). A diagram to detect serial dependencies: An application to transport time series. *Qual. Quant.*, *51*, 581–594. https://doi.org/10.1007/s11135-016-0426-y.

Bashan, A., Bartsch, R., Kantelhardt, J. W., & Havlin, S. (2008). Comparison of detrending methods for fluctuation analysis. *Physica A*, *387*, 5080–5090. https://doi.org/10.1016/j.physa.2008.04.023.

Benzi, R., Ciliberto, S., Tripiccione, R., Baudet, C., Massaioli, F., & Succi, S. (1993). Extended self-similarity in turbulent flows. *Phys. Rev. E*, *48*(1), R29–R32. https://doi.org/10.1103/PhysRevE.48.R29.

Betz, F., Oprică, S., Peltonen, T. A., & Sarlin, P. (2014). Predicting distress in European banks. *J. Bank. Financ.*, *45*, 225–241. https://doi.org/10.1016/j.jbankfin.2013.11.041.

Blender, R., Fraedrich, K., & Sienz, F. (2008). Extreme event return times in long-term memory processes near 1/f. *Nonlin. Process Geophys.*, *15*(4), 557–565. https://doi.org/10.5194/npg-15-557-2008.

Bogachev, M. I., & Bunde, A. (2008). Memory effects in the statistics of interoccurrence times between large returns in financial records. *Phys. Rev. E*, *78*(3), 036114. https://doi.org/10.1103/PhysRevE.78.036114.

Bogachev, M. I., & Bunde, A. (2009a). Improved risk estimation in multifractal records: Application to the value at risk in finance. *Phys. Rev. E*, *80*(2), 026131. https://doi.org/10.1103/PhysRevE.80.026131.

Bogachev, M. I., & Bunde, A. (2009b). On the occurrence and predictability of overloads in telecommunication networks. *EPL (Europhys. Lett.)*, *86*, 66002. https://doi.org/10.1209/0295-5075/86/66002.

Bogachev, M. I., & Bunde, A. (2011). On the predictability of extreme events in records with linear and nonlinear long-range memory: Efficiency and noise robustness. *Physica A*, *390*, 2240–2250. https://doi.org/10.1016/j.physa.2011.02.024.

Bogachev, M. I., Eichner, J. F., & Bunde, A. (2007). Effect of nonlinear correlations on the statistics of return intervals in multifractal data sets. *Phys. Rev. Lett.*, *99*(24), 240601. https://doi.org/10.1103/PhysRevLett.99.240601.

Bogachev, M. I., Eichner, J. F., & Bunde, A. (2008a). The effects of multifractality on the statistics of return intervals. *Eur. Phys. J. - Spec. Top.*, *161*, 181–193. https://doi.org/10.1140/epjst/e2008-00760-5.

Bogachev, M. I., Eichner, J. F., & Bunde, A. (2008b). On the occurrence of extreme events in long-term correlated and multifractal data sets. *Pure Appl. Geophys.*, *165*, 1195–1207. https://doi.org/10.1007/s00024-008-0353-5.

Bollen, B., & Inder, B. (2002). Estimating daily volatility in financial markets utilizing intraday data. *J. Empir. Financ.*, *9*(5), 551–562. https://doi.org/10.1016/S0927-5398(02)00010-5.

Bollerslev, T. (1986). Generalized autoregressive conditional heteroskedasticity. *J. Econometr.*, *31*(3), 307–327. https://doi.org/10.1016/0304-4076(86)90063-1.

Bunde, A., Bogachev, M. I., & Lennartz, S. (2012). Precipitation and river flow: Long-term memory and predictability of extreme events. In A. S. Sharma, A. Bunde, V. P. Dimri, & D. N. Baker (eds.), *Extreme Events and Natural Hazards: The Complexity Perspective* (pp. 139–152). Berlin: AGU Geophysical Monograph Series.

Bunde, A., Eichner, J. F., Havlin, S., & Kantelhardt, J. W. (2003). The effect of long-term correlations on the return periods of rare events. *Physica A, 330*, 1–7. https://.org/10.1016/j.physa.2003.08.004.

Bunde, A., Eichner, J. F., Havlin, S., & Kantelhardt, J. W. (2004). Return intervals of rare events in records with long-term persistence. *Physica A, 342*, 308–314. https://doi.org/10.1016/j.physa.2004.01.069

Bunde, A., Eichner, J. F., Kantelhardt, J. W., & Havlin, S. (2005). Long-term memory: A natural mechanism for the clustering of extreme events and anomalous residual times in climate records. *Phys. Rev. Lett., 94*, 048701. https://doi.org/10.1103/PhysRevLett.94.048701.

Bunde, A., & Lennartz, S. (2012). Long-term correlations in earth sciences. *Acta Geophys., 60*(3), 562–588. https://doi.org/10.2478/s11600-012-0034-8.

Carbone, A. (2009). Detrending moving average algorithm: A brief review. 2009 IEEE Toronto International Conference *Science and Technology for Humanity (TIC-STH)*, 691–696. https://doi.org/10.1109/TICSTH .2009.5444412.

Carbone, A., & Castelli, G. (2003). Scaling properties of long-range correlated noisy signals: Appplication to financial markets. *Proc. SPIE, 5114*, 406–414. https://doi.org/10.1117/12.497039.

Carbone, A., Castelli, G., & Stanley, H. E. (2004a). Analysis of clusters formed by the moving average of a long-range correlated time series. *Phys. Rev. E, 69*(2), 026105. https://doi.org/10.1103/PhysRevE.69.026105.

Carbone, A., Castelli, G., & Stanley, H. E. (2004b). Time-dependent Hurst exponent in financial time series. *Physica A, 344*(1–2), 267–271. https://doi.org/10.1016/j.physa.2004.06.130.

Castro e Silva, A., & Moreira, J. G. (1997). Roughness exponents to calculate multi-affine fractal exponents. *Physica A, 235*(3), 327–333. https://doi.org/10.1016/S0378-4371(96)00357-3.

Chen, Z., Ivanov, P. C., Hu, K., & Stanley, H. E. (2002). Effect of nonstationarities on detrended fluctuation analysis. *Phys. Rev. E, 65*(4), 041107. https://doi.org/10.1103/PhysRevE.65.041107.

Chicheportiche, R., & Chakraborti, A. (2014). Copulas and time series with long-ranged dependencies. *Phys. Rev. E, 89*(4), 042117. https://doi.org/10 .1103/PhysRevE.89.042117.

Chicheportiche, R., & Chakraborti, A. (2017). A model-free characterization of recurrences in stationary time series. *Physica A, 474*, 312–318. https://doi .org/10.1016/j.physa.2017.01.073.

Christensen, I., & Li, F.- C. (2014). Predicting financial stress events: A signal extraction approach. *J. Financ. Stabil., 14*, 54–65. https://doi.org/10.1016/j .jfs.2014.08.005.

Clauset, A., Shalizi, C. R., & Newman, M. E. J. (2009). Power-law distributions in empirical data. *SIAM Rev.*, *51*(4), 661–703. https://doi.org/10.1137/070710111.

Dai, Y.- H., Jiang, Z.- Q., & Zhou, W.- X. (2018). Forecasting extreme atmospheric events with a recurrence-interval-analysis-based autoregressive conditional duration model. *Sci. Rep.*, *8*, 16264. https://doi.org/10.1038/s41598-018-34584-4.

Deng, W., & Wang, J. (2015). Statistical analysis on multifractal detrended cross-correlation coefficient for return interval by oriented percolation. *Int. J. Mod. Phys. C*, *26*(1), 1550002. https://doi.org/10.1142/S0129183115500023.

Dong, Y. F., & Wang, J. (2013). Fluctuation behavior of financial return interval series model for percolation on Sierpinski carpet lattice. *Fractals*, *21*(3–4), 1350023. https://doi.org/10.1142/S0218348X13500230.

Drożdż, S., Kwapień, J., Oświęcimka, P., & Rak, R. (2009). Quantitative features of multifractal subtleties in time series. *EPL (Europhys. Lett.)*, *88*(6), 60003. https://doi.org/10.1209/0295-5075/88/60003.

Duca, M. L., & Peltonen, T. A. (2013). Assessing systemic risks and predicting systemic events. *J. Bank. Financ.*, *37*(7), 2183–2195. https://doi.org/10.1016/j.jbankfin.2012.06.010.

Eichner, J. F., Kantelhardt, J. W., Bunde, A., & Havlin, S. (2007). Statistics of return intervals in long-term correlated records. *Phys. Rev. E*, *75*(1), 011128. https://doi.org/10.1103/PhysRevE.75.011128.

Eisler, Z., & Kertész, J. (2006). Size matters: Some stylized facts of the stock market revisited. *Eur. Phys. J. B*, *51*(1), 145–154. https://doi.org/10.1140/epjb/e2006-00189-6.

El-Shagi, M., Knedlik, T., & von Schweinitz, G. (2013). Predicting financial crises: The (statistical) significance of the signals approach. *J. Int. Money Financ.*, *35*, 76–103. https://doi.org/10.1016/j.jimonfin.2013.02.001.

Engle, R. F., & Russell, J. R. (1998). Autoregressive conditional duration: A new model for irregularly spaced transaction data. *Econometrica*, *66*(5), 1127–1162. https://doi.org/10.2307/2999632.

Fawcett, T. (2006). An introduction to roc analysis. *Pattern Recognit. Lett.*, *27*(8), 861–874. https://doi.org/10.1016/j.patrec.2005.10.010.

Filimonov, V., Wheatley, S., & Sornette, D. (2015). Effective measure of endogeneity for the autoregressive conditional duration point processes via mapping to the self-excited Hawkes process. *Commun. Nonlinear Sci. Numer. Simul.*, *22*(1–3), 23–37. https://doi.org/10.1016/j.cnsns.2014.08.042.

Gao, X.- L., Shao, Y.- H., Yang, Y.- H., & Zhou, W.- X. (2022). Do the global grain spot markets exhibit multifractal nature? *Chaos Solitons Fractals*, *164*, 112663. https://doi.org/10.1016/j.chaos.2022.112663.

Garman, M. B., & Klass, M. J. (1980). On the estimation of security price volatilities from historical data. *J. Business*, *53*, 67–78. https://www.jstor.org/stable/2352358

Gontis, V. (2016). Interplay between endogenous and exogenous fluctuations in financial markets. *Acta Phys. Pol. A*, *129*(5), 1023–1031. https://doi.org/10.12693/APhysPolA.129.1023.

Gontis, V., Havlin, S., Kononovicius, A., Podobnik, B., & Stanley, H. E. (2016). Stochastic model of financial markets reproducing scaling and memory in volatility return intervals. *Physica A*, *462*, 1091–1102. https://doi.org/10.1016/j.physa.2016.06.143.

González, M. C., Hidalgo, C. A., & Barabási, A.- L. (2008). Understanding individual human mobility patterns. *Nature*, *453*, 779–782. https://doi.org/10.1038/nature06958.

Gopikrishnan, P., Meyer, M., Amaral, L. A. N., & Stanley, H. E. (1998). Inverse cubic law for the distribution of stock price variations. *Eur. Phys. J. B*, *3*(2), 139–140. https://doi.org/10.1007/s100510050292.

Gresnigt, F., Kole, E., & Franses, P. H. (2015). Interpreting financial market crashes as earthquakes: A new early warning system for medium term crashes. *J. Bank. Financ.*, *56*, 123–139. https://doi.org/10.1016/j.jbankfin.2015.03.003.

Gu, G.- F., Chen, W., & Zhou, W.- X. (2008). Empirical distributions of Chinese stock returns at different microscopic timescales. *Physica A*, *387*(2–3), 495–502. https://doi.org/10.1016/j.physa.2007.10.012.

Gu, G.- F., & Zhou, W.- X. (2009). Emergence of long memory in stock volatility from a modified Mike-Farmer model. *EPL (Europhys. Lett.)*, *86*(4), 48002. https://doi.org/10.1209/0295-5075/86/48002.

Gu, G.- F., & Zhou, W.- X. (2010). Detrending moving average algorithm for multifractals. *Phys. Rev. E*, *82*(1), 011136. https://doi.org/10.1103/PhysRevE.82.011136.

Harris, L. (1986). A transaction data study of weekly and intradaily patterns in stock returns. *J. Financ. Econ.*, *16*(1), 99–117. https://doi.org/10.1016/0304-405X(86)90044-9.

Hautsch, N. (2003). Assessing the risk of liquidity suppliers on the basis of excess demand intensities. *J. Financ. Econometr.*, *1*(2), 189–215. https://doi.org/10.1093/jjfinec/nbg010.

He, L.- Y., & Chen, S.- P. (2011). A new approach to quantify power-law cross-correlation and its application to crude oil markets. *Physica A*, *390*(21), 3806–3814. https://doi.org/10.1016/j.physa.2011.06.013.

Helmstetter, A., & Sornette, D. (2002a). Diffusion of epicenters of earthquake aftershocks, Omori's law, and generalized continuous-time random walk models. *Phys. Rev. E, 66*(6), 061104. https://doi.org/10.1103/PhysRevE .66.061104.

Helmstetter, A., & Sornette, D. (2002b). Subcritical and supercritical regimes in epidemic models of earthquake aftershocks. *J. Geophys. Res., 107*(B10), 2237. https://doi.org/10.1029/2001JB001580

Heneghan, C., & McDarby, G. (2000). Establishing the relation between detrended fluctuation analysis and power spectral density analysis for stochastic processes. *Phys. Rev. E, 62*, 6103–6110. https://doi.org/ 10.1103/PhysRevE.62.6103

Hill, B. M. (1975). A simple general approach to inference about the tail of a distribution. *Ann. Statist., 3*, 1163–1174. https://doi.org/10.1214/ aos/1176343247

Hong, B. H., Lee, K. E., & Lee, J. W. (2007). Power law of quiet time distribution in the Korean stock-market. *Physica A, 377*(2), 576–582. https: //doi.org/10.1016/j.physa.2006.11.076.

Hu, K., Ivanov, P. C., Chen, Z., Carpena, P., & Stanley, H. E. (2001). Effect of trends on detrended fluctuation analysis. *Phys. Rev. E, 64*(1), 011114. https: //doi.org/10.1103/PhysRevE.64.011114.

Hurst, H. E. (1951). Long-term storage capacity of reservoirs. *Trans. Amer. Soc. Civil Eng., 116*, 770–808. https://doi.org/10.1061/TACEAT.0006518

Jeon, W., Moon, H.- T., Oh, G., Yang, J.- S., & Jung, W.- S. (2010). Return intervals analysis of the Korean stock market. *J. Korean Phys. Soc., 56*(3), 922–925. https://doi.org/10.3938/jkps.56.922.

Ji, L.-J., Zhou, W.-X., Liu, H.-F. et al. (2009). R/S method for unevenly sampled time series: Application to detecting long-term temporal dependence of droplets transiting through a fixed spatial point in gas-liquid two-phase turbulent jets. *Physica A, 388*(17), 3345–3354. https://doi.org/10.1016/j .physa.2009.05.006.

Jiang, Z.- Q., Canabarro, A., Podobnik, B., Stanley, H. E., & Zhou, W.- X. (2016). Early warning of large volatilities based on recurrence interval analysis in Chinese stock markets. *Quant. Financ., 16*(11), 1713–1724. https: //doi.org/10.1080/14697688.2016.1175656.

Jiang, Z.-Q., Wang, G.-J., Canabarro, A. et al. (2018). Short term prediction of extreme returns based on the recurrence interval analysis. *Quant. Financ., 18*(3), 353–370. https://doi.org/10.1080/14697688.2017.1373843.

Jiang, Z.- Q., Xie, W.- J., & Zhou, W.- X. (2014). Testing the weak-form efficiency of the WTI crude oil futures market. *Physica A, 405*, 235–244. https://doi.org/10.1016/j.physa.2014.02.042.

Jiang, Z.- Q., Xie, W.- J., Zhou, W.- X., & Sornette, D. (2019). Multifractal analysis of financial markets: A review. *Rep. Prog. Phys.*, *82*(12), 125901. https://doi.org/10.1088/1361-6633/ab42fb.

Jung, W.-S., Wang, F.-Z., Havlin, S. et al. (2008). Volatility return intervals analysis of the Japanese market. *Eur. Phys. J. B*, *62*, 113–119. https://doi.org/10.1140/epjb/e2008-00123-0.

Kaizoji, T., & Kaizoji, M. (2004). Power law for the calm-time interval of price changes. *Physica A*, *336*(3–4), 563–570. https://doi.org/10.1016/j.physa.2003.12.054.

Kantelhardt, J. W., Koscielny-Bunde, E., Rego, H. H. A., Havlin, S., & Bunde, A. (2001). Detecting long-range correlations with detrended fluctuation analysis. *Physica A*, *295*(3–4), 441–454. https://doi.org/10.1016/S0378-4371(01)00144-3.

Kantelhardt, J. W., Zschiegner, S. A., Koscielny-Bunde, E. et al. (2002). Multifractal detrended fluctuation analysis of nonstationary time series. *Physica A*, *316*(1–4), 87–114. https://doi.org/10.1016/S0378-4371(02)01383-3.

Kitt, R., & Kalda, J. (2005). Properties of low-variability periods in financial time series. *Physica A*, *345*(3–4), 622–634. https://doi.org/10.1016/j.physa.2004.07.015.

Kolmogorov, A. N. (1933). Sulla determinazione empirica di una legge di distribuzione. *Giorn. Ist. Ital. Attuar.*, *4*(1), 83–91. (Translated in English as "On the empirical determination of a distribution law" in A. N. Shiryayev (ed.), Selected Works of A. N. Kolmogorov, 139–146, Springer, 1992) https://doi.org/10.1007/978-94-011-2260-3_15.

Laherrère, J., & Sornette, D. (1998). Stretched exponential distributions in nature and economy: "Fat tails" with characteristic scales. *Eur. Phys. J. B*, *2*(4), 525–539. https://doi.org/10.1007/s100510050276.

Lee, J., Lee, K., & Rikvold, P. (2006). Waiting-time distribution for Korean stock-market index KOSPI. *J. Korean Phys. Soc.*, *48*, S123–S126. https://www.jkps.or.kr/journal/view.html?uid=7698&vmd=Full

Lennartz, S., Livina, V., Bunde, A., & Havlin, S. (2008). Long-term memory in earthquakes and the distribution of interoccurrence times. *EPL (Europhys. Lett.)*, *81*, 69001. https://doi.org/10.1209/0295-5075/81/69001.

Li, W., Wang, F., Havlin, S., & Stanley, H. E. (2011). Financial factor influence on scaling and memory of trading volume in stock market. *Phys. Rev. E*, *84*(4), 046112. https://doi.org/10.1103/PhysRevE.84.046112.

Li, W.- S., & Liaw, S.- S. (2015). Return volatility interval analysis of stock indexes during a financial crash. *Physica A*, *434*, 151-163. https://doi.org/10.1016/j.physa.2015.03.063.

Li, W.- Z., Zhai, J.- R., Jiang, Z.- Q., Wang, G.- J., & Zhou, W.- X. (2022). Predicting tail events in a RIA-EVT-copula framework. *Physica A, 600*, 127524. https://doi.org/10.1016/j.physa.2022.127524.

Liu, C., Jiang, Z.- Q., Ren, F., & Zhou, W.- X. (2009). Scaling and memory in the return intervals of energy dissipation rate in three-dimensional fully developed turbulence. *Phys. Rev. E, 80*(4), 046304. https://doi.org/10.1103/PhysRevE.80.046304.

Livina, V. N., Havlin, S., & Bunde, A. (2005). Memory in the occurrence of earthquakes. *Phys. Rev. Lett., 95*, 208501. https://doi.org/10.1103/PhysRevLett.95.208501.

Livina, V. N., Tuzov, S., Havlin, S., & Bunde, A. (2005). Recurrence intervals between earthquakes strongly depend on history. *Physica A, 348*, 591–595. https://doi.org/10.1016/j.physa.2004.08.032.

Ljung, G. M., & Box, G. E. P. (1978). On a measure of lack of fit in time series models. *Biometrika, 65*(2), 297–303. https://doi.org/10.1093/biomet/65.2.297.

Lo, A. W. (1991). Long-term memory in stock market prices. *Econometrica, 59*, 1279–1313. https://doi.org/10.2307/2938368

Lo, A. W., & Wang, J. (2000). Trading volume: Definitions, data analysis, and implications of portfolio theory. *Rev. Financ. Stud., 13*(2), 257–300. https://doi.org/10.1093/rfs/13.2.257.

Luc, B., & Pierre, G. (2000). The logarithmic ACD model: An application to the bid-ask quote process of three NYSE stocks. *Annales d'Économie et de Statistique, 60*(60), 117–149. https://doi.org/10.2307/20076257.

Ludescher, J., & Bunde, A. (2014). Universal behavior of the interoccurrence times between losses in financial markets: Independence of the time resolution. *Phys. Rev. E, 90*(6), 062809. https://doi.org/10.1103/PhysRevE.90.062809.

Ludescher, J., Tsallis, C., & Bunde, A. (2011). Universal behaviour of interoccurrence times between losses in financial markets: An analytical description. *EPL (Europhys.Lett.), 95*(6), 68002. https://doi.org/10.1209/0295-5075/95/68002.

Lunde, A. (1999). *A Generalized Gamma Autoregressive Conditional Duration Model*. (Working paper)

Malevergne, Y., Pisarenko, V., & Sornette, D. (2005). Empirical distributions of stock returns: Between the stretched exponential and the power law? *Quant. Financ., 5*(4), 379–401. https://doi.org/10.1080/14697680500151343.

Malevergne, Y., & Sornette, D. (2006). *Extreme Financial Risks: From Dependence to Risk Management*. Berlin: Springer.

Mandelbrot, B. B., & Wallis, J. R. (1969a). Computer experiments with fractional Gaussian noise. Part 2, rescaled ranges and spectra. *Water Resour. Res.*, *5*, 242–259. https://doi.org/10.1029/WR005i001p00228

Mandelbrot, B. B., & Wallis, J. R. (1969b). Robustness of the rescaled range R/S in the measurement of noncyclic long run statistical dependence. *Water Resour. Res.*, *5*, 967–988. https://doi.org/10.1029/WR005i005p00967

Matsushita, R., Gleria, I., Figueiredo, A., & Silva, S. D. (2007). Are pound and euro the same currency? *Phys. Lett. A*, *368*(3–4), 173–180. https://doi.org/10.1016/j.physleta.2007.03.085.

Meng, H., Ren, F., Gu, G.-F. et al. (2012). Effects of long memory in the order submission process on the properties of recurrence intervals of large price fluctuations. *EPL (Europhys.Lett.)*, *98*(3), 38003. https://doi.org/10.1209/0295-5075/98/38003.

Mike, S., & Farmer, J. D. (2008). An empirical behavioral model of liquidity and volatility. *J. Econ. Dyn. Control*, *32*(1), 200–234. https://doi.org/10.1016/j.jedc.2007.01.025.

Moloney, N. R., & Davidsen, J. (2009). Extreme value statistics and return intervals in long-range correlated uniform deviates. *Phys. Rev. E*, *79*, 041131. https://doi.org/10.1103/PhysRevE.79.041131.

Montanari, A., Taqqu, M. S., & Teverovsky, V. (1999). Estimating long-range dependence in the presence of periodicity: An empirical study. *Math. Comput. Model.*, *29*(10–12), 217–228. https://doi.org/10.1016/S0895-7177(99)00104-1.

Mu, G.-H., & Zhou, W.-X. (2010). Tests of nonuniversality of the stock return distributions in an emerging market. *Phys. Rev. E*, *82*(6), 066103. https://doi.org/10.1103/PhysRevE.82.066103.

Newey, W. K., & West, K. D. (1987). A simple, positive semi-definite, heteroskedasticity and autocorrelation consistent covariance matrix. *Econometrica*, *55*(3), 703–708. https://doi.org/10.2307/1913610.

Ng, K., Peiris, S., & Gerlach, R. (2014). Estimation and forecasting with logarithmic autoregressive conditional duration models: A comparative study with an application. *Expert Sys. Appl.*, *41*(7), 3323–3332. https://doi.org/10.1016/j.eswa.2013.11.024.

Olla, P. (2007). Return times for stochastic processes with power-law scaling. *Phys. Rev. E*, *76*, 011122. https://doi.org/10.1103/PhysRevE.76.011122

Openshaw, S., & Connolly, C. J. (1977). Empirically derived deterrence functions for maximum performance spatial interaction models. *Environ. Planning A*, *9*(9), 1068–1079. https://doi.org/10.1068/a091067.

Oświęcimka, P., Drożdż, S., Kwapień, J., & Górski, A. Z. (2013). Effect of detrending on multifractal characteristics. *Acta Phys. Pol. A*, *123*(3), 597–603. https://doi.org/10.12693/APhysPolA.123.597.

Ouyang, F. Y., Zheng, B., & Jiang, X. F. (2014). Spatial and temporal structures of four financial markets in greater China. *Physica A*, *402*, 236–244. https://doi.org/10.1016/j.physa.2014.02.006.

Pearson, E. S., & Stephens, M. A. (1962). The goodness-of-fit tests on W_N^2 and U_N^2. *Biometrika*, *49*, 397–402. https://doi.org/10.1093/biomet/49.3-4.397

Pei, A. Q., & Wang, J. (2015). Graphic analysis and multifractal on percolation-based return interval series. *Int. J. Mod. Phys. C*, *26*(12), 1550137. https://doi.org/10.1142/S0129183115501375.

Peng, C.- K., Buldyrev, S. V., Havlin, S., Simons, M., Stanley, H. E., & Goldberger, A. L. (1994). Mosaic organization of DNA nucleotides. *Phys. Rev. E*, *49*(2), 1685–1689. https://doi.org/10.1103/PhysRevE.49.1685.

Podobnik, B., Horvatic, D., Petersen, A. M., & Stanley, H. E. (2009). Cross-correlations between volume change and price change. *Proc. Natl. Acad. Sci. U. S. A.*, *106*(52), 22079–22084. https://doi.org/10.1073/pnas.0911983106.

Press, W., Teukolsky, S., Vetterling, W., & Flannery, B. (1996). *Numerical Recipes in FORTRAN: The Art of Scientific Computing*. Cambridge: Cambridge University Press.

Press, W., Teukolsky, S. A., Vetterling, W. T., & Flannery, B. P. (2007). *Numerical Recipes: The Art of Scientific Computing* (3rd ed.). Cambridge: Cambridge University Press.

Qiu, T., Guo, L., & Chen, G. (2008). Scaling and memory effect in volatility return interval of the Chinese stock market. *Physica A*, *387*, 6812–6818. https://doi.org/10.1016/j.physa.2008.09.002.

Reboredo, J. C., Rivera-Castro, M. A., & de Assis, E. M. (2014). Power-law behaviour in time durations between extreme returns. *Quant. Financ.*, *14*(12), 2171–2183. https://doi.org/10.1080/14697688.2013.822538.

Ren, F., Gu, G.- F., & Zhou, W.- X. (2009). Scaling and memory in the return intervals of realized volatility. *Physica A*, *388*(22), 4787–4796. https://doi.org/10.1016/j.physa.2009.08.009.

Ren, F., Guo, L., & Zhou, W.- X. (2009). Statistical properties of volatility return intervals of Chinese stocks. *Physica A*, *388*(6), 881–890. https://doi.org/10.1016/j.physa.2008.12.005.

Ren, F., & Zhou, W.- X. (2008). Multiscaling behavior in the volatility return intervals of Chinese indices. *EPL (Europhys.Lett.)*, *84*(6), 68001. https://doi.org/10.1209/0295-5075/84/68001.

Ren, F., & Zhou, W.- X. (2010). Recurrence interval analysis of high-frequency financial returns and its application to risk estimation. *New J. Phys.*, *12*, 075030. https://doi.org/10.1088/1367-2630/12/7/075030.

Saichev, A., & Sornette, D. (2006). "Universal" distribution of interearthquake times explained. *Phys. Rev. Lett.*, *97*(7), 078501. https://doi.org/10.1103/PhysRevLett.97.078501.

Saichev, A., & Sornette, D. (2007). Theory of earthquake recurrence times. *J. Geophys. Res.-Solid Earth*, *112*(B4), B04313. https://doi.org/10.1029/2006JB004536.

Santhanam, M. S., & Kantz, H. (2008). Return interval distribution of extreme events and long-term memory. *Phys. Rev. E*, *78*(5), 051113. https://doi.org/10.1103/PhysRevE.78.051113.

Sarlin, P. (2013). On policymakers' loss functions and the evaluation of early warning systems. *Econ. Lett.*, *119*(1), 1–7. https://doi.org/10.1016/j.econlet.2012.12.030.

Schumann, A. Y., & Kantelhardt, J. W. (2011). Multifractal moving average analysis and test of multifractal model with tuned correlations. *Physica A*, *390*(14), 2637–2654. https://doi.org/10.1016/j.physa.2011.03.002.

Serletis, A., & Rosenberg, A. A. (2007). The Hurst exponent in energy futures prices. *Physica A*, *380*, 325–332. https://doi.org/10.1016/j.physa.2007.02.055.

Serletis, A., & Rosenberg, A. A. (2009). Mean reversion in the US stock market. *Chaos Solitons Fractals*, *40*(4), 2007–2015. https://doi.org/10.1016/j.chaos.2007.09.085.

Shao, Y.- H., Gu, G.- F., Jiang, Z.- Q., & Zhou, W.- X. (2015). Effects of polynomial trends on detrending moving average analysis. *Fractals*, *23*(3), 1550034. https://doi.org/10.1142/S0218348X15500346.

Shao, Y.- H., Gu, G.- F., Jiang, Z.- Q., Zhou, W.- X., & Sornette, D. (2012). Comparing the performance of FA, DFA and DMA using different synthetic long-range correlated time series. *Sci. Rep.*, *2*, 835. https://doi.org/10.1038/srep00835.

Shiller, R. J. (1981). Do stock prices move too much to be justified by subsequent changes in dividends? *Am. Econ. Rev.*, *71*(3), 421–436. https://doi.org/10.3386/w0456.

Smirnov, N. V. (1939). On the estimation of the discrepancy between empirical curves of distribution for two independent samples. *Bull. Math. Univ. Moscow*, *2*(2), 3–4.

Sornette, D. (2003a). Critical market crashes. *Phys. Rep.*, *378*(1), 1–98. https://doi.org/10.1016/S0370-1573(02)00634-8.

Sornette, D. (2003b). *Why Stock Markets Crash*. Princeton: Princeton University Press.

Sornette, D. (2004). *Critical Phenomena in Natural Sciences* (2nd ed.). Berlin: Springer.

Sornette, D. (2009). Dragon-kings, black swans and the prediction of crises. *Int. J. Terraspace Sci. Eng.*, *2*, 1–18.

Sornette, D., & Knopoff, L. (1997). The paradox of the expected time until the next earthquake. *Bull. Seism. Soc. Am.*, *87*, 789–798. https://doi.org/10.1785/BSSA0870040789

Sornette, D., & Ouillon, G. (2012). Dragon-kings: Mechanisms, statistical methods and empirical evidence. *Eur. Phys. J.-Spec. Top.*, *205*(1), 1–26. https://doi.org/10.1140/epjst/e2012-01559-5.

Stephens, M. A. (1964). The distribution of the goodness-of-fit statistic, U_N^2. II. *Biometrika*, *51*, 393–397. https://doi.org/10.1093/biomet/51.3-4.393

Stephens, M. A. (1970). Use of the Kolmogorov-Smirnov, Cramér-Von Mises and related statistics without extensive tables. *J. R. Stat. Soc. B*, *32*(1), 115–122. https://doi.org/10.1111/j.2517-6161.1970.tb00821.x

Stephens, M. A. (1974). EDF statistics for goodness of fit and some comparisons. *J. Am. Stat. Assoc.*, *69*, 730–737. https://doi.org/10.1080/01621459.1974.10480196

Suo, Y.- Y., Wang, D.- H., & Li, S.- P. (2015). Risk estimation of CSI 300 index spot and futures in China from a new perspective. *Econ. Model.*, *49*, 344–353. https://doi.org/10.1016/j.econmod.2015.05.011.

Talkner, P., & Weber, R. O. (2000). Power spectrum and detrended fluctuation analysis: Application to daily temperatures. *Phys. Rev. E*, *62*, 150–160. https://doi.org/10.1103/PhysRevE.62.150

Taqqu, M. S., Teverovsky, V., & Willinger, W. (1995). Estimators for long-range dependence: An empirical study. *Fractals*, *3*(4), 785–798. https://doi.org/10.1142/S0218348X95000692.

Teverovsky, V., Taqqu, M. S., & Willinger, W. (1999). A critical look at Lo's modified R/S statistic. *J. Stat. Plann. Inference*, *80*, 211–227. https://doi.org/10.1016/S0378-3758(98)00250-X

Vandewalle, N., & Ausloos, M. (1998). Crossing of two mobile averages: A method for measuring the roughness exponent. *Phys. Rev. E*, *58*(5), 6832–6834. https://doi.org/10.1103/PhysRevE.58.6832.

Varotsos, P. A., Sarlis, N. V., Tanaka, H. K., & Skordas, E. S. (2005). Some properties of the entropy in the natural time. *Phys. Rev. E*, *71*(3), 032102. https://doi.org/10.1103/PhysRevE.71.032102.

Vodenska-Chitkushev, I., Wang, F.- Z., Weber, P., Yamasaki, K., Havlin, S., & Stanley, H. E. (2008). Comparison between volatility return intervals of the S&P 500 index and two common models. *Eur. Phys. J. B*, *61*, 217–223. https://doi.org/10.1140/epjb/e2008-00066-4.

Wang, F., Weber, P., Yamasaki, K., Havlin, S., & Stanley, H. E. (2007). Statistical regularities in the return intervals of volatility. *Eur. Phys. J. B*, *55*, 123–133. https://doi.org/10.1140/epjb/e2006-00356-9.

Wang, F., Yamasaki, K., Havlin, S., & Stanley, H. (2006). Scaling and memory of intraday volatility return intervals in stock markets. *Phys. Rev. E*, *73*(2), 026117. https://doi.org/10.1103/PhysRevE.73.026117.

Wang, F., Yamasaki, K., Havlin, S., & Stanley, H. E. (2008). Indication of multiscaling in the volatility return intervals of stock markets. *Phys. Rev. E*, *77*(1), 016109. https://doi.org/10.1103/PhysRevE.77.016109.

Wang, F.- Z., Yamasaki, K., Havlin, S., & Stanley, H. E. (2009). Multifactor analysis of multiscaling in volatility return intervals. *Phys. Rev. E*, *79*, 016103.https://doi.org/10.1103/PhysRevE.79.016103.

Weber, P., Wang, F., Vodenska-Chitkushev, I., Havlin, S., & Stanley, H. E. (2007). Relation between volatility correlations in financial markets and Omori processes occurring on all scales. *Phys. Rev. E*, *76*(1), 016109. https://doi.org/10.1103/PhysRevE.76.016109.

Weber, R. O., & Talkner, P. (2001). Spectra and correlations of climate data from days to decades. *J. Geophys. Res.*, *106*, 20131–20144. https://doi.org/10.1029/2001GL014170.

Wehrli, A., & Sornette, D. (2022). The excess volatility puzzle explained by financial noise amplification from endogenous feedbacks. *Sci. Rep.*, *12*(1), 18895. https://doi.org/10.1038/s41598-022-20879-0.

Wood, R. A., McInish, T. H., & Ord, J. K. (1985). An investigation of transactions data for NYSE stocks. *J. Financ.*, *40*(3), 723–739. https://doi.org/10.2307/2327796.

Wu, G.-H., Qiu, L., Stephen, M., et al., (2014). Statistics of extreme events in Chinese stock markets. *Chin. Phys. B*, *23*(12), 128901. https://doi.org/10.1088/1674-1056/23/12/128901.

Xie, W.- J., Jiang, Z.- Q., & Zhou, W.- X. (2014). Extreme value statistics and recurrence intervals of NYMEX energy futures volatility. *Econ. Model.*, *36*, 8–17. https://doi.org/10.1016/j.econmod.2013.09.011.

Xu, L. M., Ivanov, P. C., Hu, K. et al. (2005). Quantifying signals with power-law correlations: A comparative study of detrended fluctuation analysis and detrended moving average techniques. *Phys. Rev. E*, *71*(21), 051101. https://doi.org/10.1103/PhysRevE.71.051101.

Yakovlev, G., Turcotte, D. L., Rundle, J. B., & Rundle, P. B. (2006). Simulation-based distributions of earthquake recurrence times on the San Andreas fault system. *Bull. Seismol. Soc. Amer.*, *96*(6), 1995–2007. https://doi.org/10.1785/0120050183.

Yamasaki, K., Muchnik, L., Havlin, S., Bunde, A., & Stanley, H. E. (2005). Scaling and memory in volatility return intervals in financial markets. *Proc. Natl. Acad. Sci. U. S. A.*, *102*(26), 9424–9428. https://doi.org/10.1073/pnas.0502613102.

Yamasaki, K., Muchnik, L., Havlin, S., Bunde, A., & Stanley, H. E. (2006). Scaling and memory in return loss intervals: Application to risk estimation. In H. Takayasu (ed.), *Practical Fruits of Econophysics* (pp. 43–51). Berlin: Springer-Verlag. https://doi.org/10.1007/4-431-28915-1_7.

Yang, G., & Wang, J. (2016). Complexity and multifractal of volatility duration for agent-based financial dynamics and real markets. *Fractals*, *24*(4), 1650052. https://doi.org/10.1142/S0218348X16500523.

Yuan, Y., Zhuang, X.- t., Liu, Z.- y., & Huang, W.- q. (2014). Analysis of the temporal properties of price shock sequences in crude oil markets. *Physica A*, *394*, 235–246. https://doi.org/10.1016/j.physa.2013.09.040.

Zhang, C., Pu, Z., & Zhou, Q. (2018). Sustainable energy consumption in northeast Asia: A case from China's fuel oil futures market. *Sustainability*, *10*(1), 261. https://doi.org/10.3390/su10010261.

Zhang, J.- H., Wang, J., & Shao, J.- G. (2010). Finite-range contact process on the market return intervals distributions. *Adv. Complex Sys.*, *13*, 643–657. https://doi.org/10.1142/S0219525910002797.

Zhao, X., Shang, P., & Lin, A. (2016). Universal and non-universal properties of recurrence intervals of rare events. *Physica A*, *448*, 132–143. https://doi.org/10.1016/j.physa.2015.12.082.

Zhou, W.- J., Wang, Z.- X., & Guo, H.- M. (2016). Modelling volatility recurrence intervals in the Chinese commodity futures market. *Physica A*, *457*, 514–525. https://doi.org/10.1016/j.physa.2016.03.044.

Zhou, W.- J., Wu, X.- L., Pan, J., & Wang, Z.- X. (2020). Recurrence intervals analysis of CSI 300 future based on high frequency data. *Econ. Comput. Econ. Cybern. Stud.*, *54*(2), 299–314. https://doi.org/10.24818/18423264/54.2.20.18.

Zhou, W.- X. (2009). The components of empirical multifractality in financial returns. *EPL (Europhys.Lett.)*, *88*(2), 28004. https://doi.org/10.1209/0295-5075/88/28004.

Zhou, W.- X. (2012a). Determinants of immediate price impacts at the trade level in an emerging order-driven market. *New J. Phys.*, *14*, 023055. https://doi.org/10.1088/1367-2630/14/2/023055.

Zhou, W.- X. (2012b). Finite-size effect and the components of multifractality in financial volatility. *Chaos Solitons Fractals*, *45*(2), 147–155. https://doi.org/10.1016/j.chaos.2011.11.004.

Zhou, W.- X. (2012c). Universal price impact functions of individual trades in an order-driven market. *Quant. Financ.*, *12*(8), 1253–1263. https://doi.org /10.1080/14697688.2010.504733.

Zhou, W.- X., Sornette, D., & Yuan, W.- K. (2006). Inverse statistics and multifractality of exit distances in 3D fully developed turbulence. *Physica D*, *214*(1), 55–62. doi: https://doi.org/10.1016/j.physd.2005.12.004.

Acknowledgments

We thank our collaborators Askery Canabarro (Universidade Federal de Alagoas), Yue-Hua Dai (Development Research Center of the Shanghai Municipal Peoples Government), Gao-Feng Gu (East China University of Science and Technology), Liang Guo, Wei-Zhen Li, Hao Meng, Boris Podobnik (University of Rijeka), Fei Ren (East China University of Science and Technology), H. Eugene Stanley (Boston University), Gangjin Wang (Hunan University), Chi Xie (Hunan University), and Jin-Rui Zhai. We also thank Series Editor Rosario Nunzio Mantegna and two referees. We acknowledge financial supports from the National Natural Science of Foundation of China (U1811462 and 72171083), the Shanghai Outstanding Academic Leaders Plan, and the Fundamental Research Funds for the Central Universities.

Cambridge Elements ≡

Econophysics

Rosario Nunzio Mantegna

University of Palermo

Rosario Nunzio Mantegna is Professor of Applied Physics at the University of Palermo and an external faculty member of the Complexity Science Hub in Vienna. He is one of the pioneers of econophysics and economic networks, and he co-authored the first book on the topic ('Introduction to Econophysics', Cambridge, 1999).

Bikas K. Chakrabarti

Saha Institute of Nuclear Physics

Bikas K. Chakrabarti is Emeritus Professor at Saha Institute of Nuclear Physics and visiting Professor of Economics in the Indian Statistical Institute, Kolkata. He has co-authored more than two hundred papers and ten books (including 'Econophysics of Income & Wealth Distributions', Cambridge, 2013). In 1995, he organized a conference in Kolkata, where the term "econophysics" was first coined.

Mauro Gallegati

Università Politecnica delle Marche

Mauro Gallegati is Professor of Economics at the Polytechnic University of Marche, Ancona. He has previously held visiting scholarships at Cambridge, Stanford, MIT, Columbia, the Santa Fe Institute, the Brookings Institution, and ETH Zurich. His research includes business fluctuations, nonlinear dynamics, models of financial fragility, and heterogeneous interacting agents.

Irena Vodenska

Boston University

Irena Vodenska is Professor and Director of Finance Programs at Boston University Metropolitan College. Her research is focused on network theory and complexity science in macroeconomics, particularly the modeling of early warning indicators and systemic risk propagation throughout interconnected financial and economic networks. She is a co-editor of the book 'Econophysics and Sociophysics: Recent Progress and Future Directions' (Springer, 2017)

About the Series

The readership of this Element series consists of (i) physicists interested in the description and modelling of economic complex systems, (ii) economists who want to consider a data-driven and computational-driven approach, and (iii) practitioners working in the financial industry (especially those of them that are quantitative by training).

Cambridge Elements ≡

Econophysics

Elements in the Series

Recurrence Interval Analysis of Financial Time Series
Wei-Xing Zhou, Zhi-Qiang Jiang, and Wen-Jie Xie

A full series listing is available at: www.cambridge.org/EECP

Printed in the United States
by Baker & Taylor Publisher Services